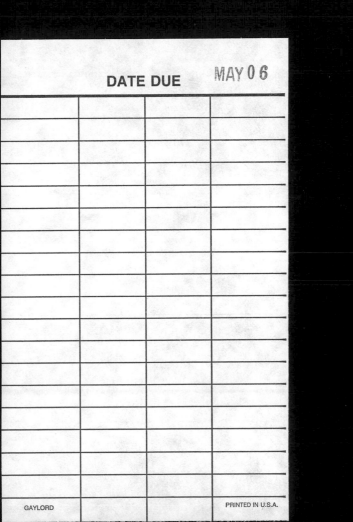

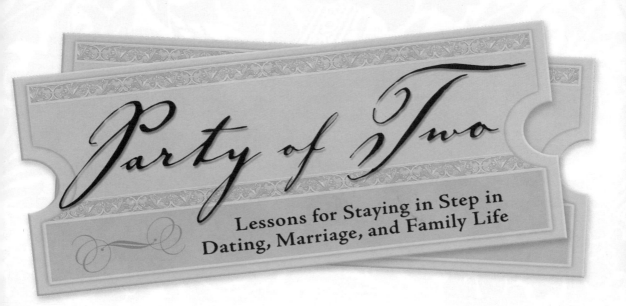

Party of Two

Lessons for Staying in Step in Dating, Marriage, and Family Life

Tim & Beverly LaHaye

New Leaf Press
A Division of New Leaf Publishing Group

Party of Two

First Printing: February 2006

ISBN 13: 978-0-89221-638-3
ISBN 10: 0-89221-638-7
Library of Congress Control Number: 2005938405

Published in association with the literary agency of Alive Communications, Inc., 1465 Kelly Johnson Blvd., Ste. 320, Colorado Springs, CO 80920.

Cover design by Janell Robertson
Interior design by Rebekah Krall

Printed in the United States of America

Please visit our website for other great titles:
www.newleafpress.net

For information regarding author interviews,
please contact the publicity department at (870) 438-5288.

New Leaf Press
A Division of New Leaf Publishing Group

Contents

Lilies Among Thorns

Finding the Mate God Has for You

Did you know that life's most crucial decisions will be made between the ages of 18 and 25?

During that time, you will be faced with many choices. Some will be minor decisions while others will have an impact on the rest of your life. Suppose you impulsively purchase a car without putting much prayer or thought into it. If it turns out to be a "lemon," your poor judgment may simply result in expensive repair bills and a lot of inconvenience and aggravation. Since this was a minor decision, you eventually trade in your mistake without any lasting effect on your life. Other decisions are not so easily dismissed. In fact, during the seven-year period between 18 and 25 years of age, you will make five decisions that will chart the course of your life.

How will you answer these five important questions?

Five Important Decisions

1. What will I do after I finish high school?
2. What career will I pursue?
3. Where will I live?
4. Where will I attend church?
5. Whom will I marry?

Life's Five Most Important Decisions

1. What will I do after I finish high school?

The kind of school, college, or job you choose will set your life on a course that will likely determine the kind of education you receive, how much money you will eventually earn, and the opportunities you will have in the future.

Your post-high school education — or lack of it — will affect your life's vocation. That's your second great decision.

2. What career will I pursue?

Some high school graduates know exactly what they want to do in life and begin pursuing their college or career goals immediately. Others choose to join the military or get a full-time job before deciding on a specific course of action. Some feel that God is calling them to serve Him as a pastor, church music director, youth pastor, or missionary.

As long as you find the right training ground — and are available to God to make the right decision about what to do with your life — you will eventually be headed in the right direction.

3. Where will I live?

God has a will for where you live, including your state, city, and neighborhood.

No matter where you live, you can serve the Lord.

One of our family's greatest joys has been to pray for our neighbors and see them come to know Christ as their Lord and Saviour. That's one of the best ways we as Christians can further God's kingdom.

4. Where will I attend church?

It's not about *whether* you will go to church, but *where?* This is a question you should ask God, whether you live on a college campus, on a military base, or at home with your parents.

It is important to find the right church. Look for a church where God is praised, the Bible is taught as God's Word, and Jesus is lifted up as Saviour, Lord, and soon-coming King. Then, attend every Sunday, get involved in serving your church family, and tithe your income.

5. Whom will I marry?

Don't think in terms of *will* I marry, but *whom* will I marry? I believe it is God's will for young people to marry. Whom you marry is a vital decision that will dramatically affect the course your life will take.

If you put Christ on the throne of your heart and seek His will for your life, the choices you make regarding these five decisions will set you on the right course for the rest of your life.

MAKING RIGHT CHOICES

Life is full of decisions, and making right choices is not easy. In fact, it's probably one of the hardest things to do in life. Why? Because there is a constant struggle between man's will and God's will.

1. Whom will you serve?

If your motto is: "I will do as I please," you are living according to your own will. You have chosen to ignore God's commands and have refused to place Jesus Christ on the throne of your life. As a result, all your decisions are based on your desires, your needs, and your ego.

Behind the scenes, another force is also at work. With great skill and cunning manipulation, Satan subtly tries to influence your decisions by pulling your will in his direction.

When God says, "Young man, young lady, give Me your life," Satan counters with, "Don't waste your time calling on Jesus Christ."

Ultimately, however, the decision is yours.

2. Who controls your life?

Once you have trusted Him as Saviour, you must make another decision. Will you make Jesus Lord of your life? In other words, will you submit your will to His will? This is where the battle line is drawn — at the point of your will.

If you're going to be "transformed," as the Bible says, you are going to be different. This is where the real test of your commitment to Christ takes place.

Don't be afraid to have different standards and principles. Don't worry about what other people think because you choose to dress modestly and refuse to go to nightclubs or R-rated movies. You can't live "godly in Christ Jesus" and still look and act like the devil.

Don't back off because you're different. That should be the hallmark of a Christian. The Bible calls us "a peculiar people" who are eagerly doing "good works." If you're zealously serving Jesus Christ, that's all the peculiarity you need to be different from the world.

3. How can you find God's will?

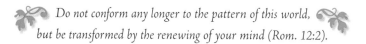

Do not conform any longer to the pattern of this world, but be transformed by the renewing of your mind (Rom. 12:2).

How do you renew your mind? By reading and studying the Word of God. That's how you will be able to test and approve what God's will is.

As a young person with your life ahead of you, it's not too late for you to find and do "the perfect will of God."

How do you find God's will? Ask Him:

In all your ways acknowledge Him, and He shall direct your paths (Prov. 3:6).

God has a will for your life. Don't settle for anything less when deciding where you will go to school, what will be your vocation, where you go to church, and whom you will marry.

The Dating Game

Dating is a phenomenon of western civilization. In fact, two-thirds of the world today follows the same custom that was practiced during Bible times: Parents select the mate for their son or daughter.

Dating, however, doesn't have to be complicated, especially if you are a Christian committed to following Christ and seeking God's will for your life. In that case, the Holy Spirit is your matchmaker. You only have to wait for Him to make a match!

In the meantime, I recommend you follow these simple suggestions.

1. Date only Christians.

What draws people together? Usually, it is some common interest. That is often followed by physical or personality attraction that leads to association, and association leads to love. Love at first sight, however, is a myth perpetrated by Hollywood.

How can you avoid becoming emotionally entangled with an unsaved person?

Cut it off at the pass. If he or she is not a Christian, don't associate with him or her in an intimate or personal way.

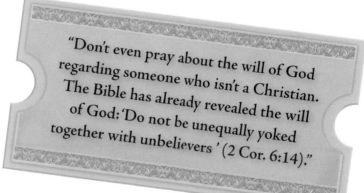

"Don't even pray about the will of God regarding someone who isn't a Christian. The Bible has already revealed the will of God: 'Do not be unequally yoked together with unbelievers' (2 Cor. 6:14)."

Don't even pray about the will of God regarding someone who isn't a Christian. The Bible has already revealed the will of God: "Do not be unequally yoked together with unbelievers" (2 Cor. 6:14).

Set this simple rule for your life: I will not date an unbeliever, and I will never marry an unbeliever. Sounds simple, but it works.

Whenever two people get together and one is a Christian and the other is not — whether it's on a courting basis or two fellows sharing a college room — one of three things will always happen:

> *A. The Christian will reach the unbeliever and lead Him to a saving knowledge of Jesus Christ. That's the best outcome.*
> *B. The unbeliever will have a souring, deadening effect upon the Christian.*
> *C. They will naturally lose interest in each other.*

Either the unsaved person will rise to the position of the Christian, and they will reach common ground, or the Christian will stoop to the level of the unbeliever, or they'll separate.

Why does it always happen this way? Because the unsaved person, "the natural man," cannot understand "the things of the Spirit of God, for they are foolishness to him; nor can he know them, because they are spiritually discerned" (1 Cor. 2:14).

2. Look for someone who can complement your particular temperament.

All of us are born with a certain type of temperament. Whether male of female, we all fall into one of four categories — or a combination of two types:

> *A. Choleric*
>
> *B. Sanguine*
>
> *C. Melancholy*
>
> *D. Phlegmatic*

Temperament is not developed as you mature or imposed on you during your upbringing. You are born with it. However, your temperament can later be adjusted by the Holy Spirit.

Whenever I walk into the nursery in our church, I am able to identify the four personality types in the little children playing there.

The choleric children have all the toys.

The sanguine kids are running around having a happy time.

The melancholy children are looking around, staring at everyone.

The phlegmatic kids are off in the corner playing all by themselves, not bothering anyone.

During the dating years, you will probably be attracted to another person of the opposite sex in an affectionate way for reasons you don't fully understand. The first infatuation may be because of looks, appeal, circumstances, or biological magnetic attraction.

Also at work is a subconscious attraction toward the strengths we admire in that person — strengths that correspond with our weaknesses.

I've never known anyone to consciously say, "I fell in love with Mary because I am an uninhibited, disorganized sanguine and she is a meticulous, careful, and neat melancholy." But that's exactly what happens.

At the same time, neat, precise Mary is attracted to sloppy Fred because he's gregarious and outgoing. But they don't realize it!

Rocky Choleric will usually fall in love with Polly Phlegmatic. Why? She's the only one who can put up with his hard-driving, dynamic personality.

After marriage, however, Rocky may turn into a caustic, cruel, sarcastic, unaffectionate character if the Holy Spirit does not get hold of him. Polly's sweet, demure, gracious, gentle, quiet spirit can turn her into a stubborn, sullen, silent, and disorganized wife.

By being aware of the strengths and weaknesses of the different personality types, you can ask the Holy Spirit to change those areas in your life that need His touch. You can also begin to pray that God will begin now to prepare the temperament of the person He has for you — so you can both complement one another.

3. Date for fun, not marriage.

Some guys approach dating much too seriously. You're afraid if you ask a girl to have cappuccino with you, she'll be planning the wedding before your cup is empty.

Girls, when a guy asks you out for the evening, don't think you're making the greatest commitment of your life. You're simply committing yourself to him for one evening, and he's committing himself to you to be a Christian gentleman. That is all; nothing more. Don't go home afterwards and start browsing through *Modern Bride* magazine.

Guys, if you meet a girl you'd like to get to know better, why not enjoy a nice, sociable evening together? Let's face it, there's something exotically inspiring about being in the company of the opposite sex. It's worth those 20 bucks you'll invest in refreshments.

My advice to young men and women: Lighten up! Enjoy each other in a casual relationship and have fun while you're dating.

4. Relax and trust the Holy Spirit.

If you're walking in the Spirit regarding your male/female encounters, you can relax and enjoy dating — or not dating.

Remember, it's the Holy Spirit's job to work everything "together for good" in your life. He picks the time, the person, and the circumstances. When you are ready, and your prospective mate is prepared, the Holy Spirit will let both of you know at the same time.

Girls need to keep in mind that some guys are simply not interested in dating. It's not that they aren't attracted to the opposite sex, it's just that they have a lot of other things on their minds.

Our society puts a lot of pressure on men to "be all that they can be." Many guys — and girls — take their lives and futures seriously. Between the ages of 18 to 22, however, a guy is more likely thinking about finishing his education, getting a job, and pursuing a career. His life is indefinite and his future uncertain. Until everything falls into place, marriage may not be high on his list of things to do.

At the same time, a young man may be afraid to date for fun. Most Christian guys try to be considerate of a girl's feelings and don't want to mislead them. Guys feel guilty if they want to date but have no intention of marrying at this point in their lives.

My suggestion to guys in this situation? Relax and let the Holy Spirit put the process of natural selection to work. The cream will rise to the top in any milk bottle.

Any person God sends into your life will bring with him or her a sense of peace, love, and joy. If he or she is the right one, you won't have to wonder. Your spirit will bear witness with the Holy Spirit that this is God's choice, and He will bring you together in His time and in His way.

5. Keep your dating relationship pure.

When I suggest that you date for fun, I'm assuming you know the difference between good, wholesome, clean Christian fun and an illegitimate "good time."

The world teaches that sex is okay as long as it is "safe." God's Word teaches that sex is okay as long as two people are married — and there are no exceptions.

If you want to keep your relationship wholesome, you must avoid the biological, magnetic attraction that the two sexes naturally have for one another. By making physical contact off-limits, you set your heart and mind free to learn more about each other in the mental and spiritual realm without the sexual distraction.

When you go out on a date as a Christian guy and a Christian girl, you want to return home knowing you have conducted yourselves in a manner worthy of Christ. The best gift you can give your date is a peaceful night's sleep with a clear conscience.

In counseling sessions, I deal with people all the time who are suffering a backlash of guilt resulting from the sin they practiced during their dating years. Don't let that be the legacy you take into your marriage. It will only come back to haunt you.

> "The world teaches that sex is okay as long as it is 'safe.' God's Word teaches that sex is okay as long as two people are married — and there are no exceptions."

6. Guys, conduct yourself as a Christian gentleman.

A girl respects a guy who respects her body and understands that she has a responsibility to God to keep herself pure. As a Christian, you should treat her like a sister in the Lord. If you really love a young lady, you're going to protect her from doing anything that would cause her to sin against God.

Be a man. Make it your goal to please one master — Jesus Christ — not the violent force of lust, passion, or free love. With the help of the Holy Spirit, you can resist any temptation. All you have to do is ask.

7. Girls, learn to say, "No!"

Don't allow yourselves to be a victim of male lust. That's the world's concept — not God's will.

You have a Heavenly Father who loves you and wants to protect your purity and virtue. Any spirit that leads you to violate the Bible's standards of modesty and sanctity is not the Holy Spirit.

"If I act too religious, I won't be popular with the boys," you may complain.

Guys have big egos, and they don't always keep confidences. As I remember, the boys in the locker room knew the difference between the girls who were trying to please the boys and the girls who had standards.

The girls who wanted to please the boys — and did — had lots of dates, but the girls who had standards were the ones who got married first. In fact, some guys will tell you anything and everything as long as they get what they want.

I know it's not easy, especially in our sexually promiscuous society. At times you will need tremendous discipline and be required to invoke a Holy Spirit-inspired "No!"

The stronger you are in the Spirit, the easier it will be to resist the sexual pressures and temptations of dating. On your wedding night, however, you will rejoice knowing you kept yourself pure for the mate God has given you.

8. Don't tempt the opposite sex with revealing clothing.

During one of my seminars, a young man handed me a piece of paper on which he had written this question: "I have a problem with a girl I've been dating. She wears very short skirts, and I'm not sure if the feeling I have for her is love or lust. Can I be filled with the Spirit and feel this way? Can she be filled with the Spirit and entice me like that?"

Many Christian women and girls do not understand the problem a man has with his eyes and his mind.

Women aren't stimulated by what they see in the same way men are.

Jesus pinpointed this issue when He said to men, "But I say to you that whoever looks at a woman to lust for her has already committed adultery with her in his heart" (Matt. 5:28).

The Lord Jesus knew what was in men, and He knows what's in women. Men have a problem with lust that women don't have.

Christian men want their eyes to be dedicated to God, but they are constantly bombarded by scenes that incite them to lust.

At the same time, Christian women and girls aren't much help. When a woman sitting in a church pew has her legs exposed far above her knees, such a sight is not conducive to a man's worship.

The apostle Paul wrote, "Therefore, if food makes my brother stumble, I will never again eat meat, lest I make my brother stumble" (1 Cor. 8:13). In other words, if my behavior or actions cause someone else to sin or to interfere with his relationship to God, then I need to change what I am doing.

Short skirts are only part of the problem. Bikinis and other revealing clothing do not belong in the wardrobe of any woman or girl who is seeking to obey God's Word and serve Jesus Christ as Lord.

9. Pray together.

"Do you really think that young people can pray together when they are dating?"

You bet I do. In fact, the most beautiful relationship in the world takes place when two human beings of the opposite sex pray together.

It's good to have a planned time to pray. Why? It's a safeguard.

In the beginning, you can pray and ask the Lord to help you please Him in all you do on your date. Then, if you know at the end of your date that you're going to have a time of prayer together, you will be conscious of where you go and how you conduct yourselves on your date.

If you can't pray together while you are dating, you need to examine your relationship to one another — and to the Lord.

10. Avoid unnecessary body contact.

Every male and female has a biological, magnetic pull toward certain members of the opposite sex, but that doesn't mean he or she is the one God has chosen for you.

If she's your number, just being in the same car with her will make your temperature rise, but that's normal. That's the way God made you. In fact, that is a natural reaction.

Take dancing for instance. Any red-blooded guy and girl who stand close while moving their bodies together to the accompaniment of throbbing, mind-numbing hip-hop music can't help but get turned on.

As for dancing in general, I would not consider it a wholesome practice for any believer who is striving to lead a godly, Christian life. In fact, anyone who uses his or her body to sexually stimulate members of the opposite sex is tempting others to sin.

Unnecessary body contact only serves to pour gasoline on your emotional fires. It only takes one touch to erase your standards and toss your good judgment out the window.

You see, we not only have the law of God, but we have a conscience that accuses us or excuses us.

Sex before marriage changes a couple's relationship forever. It is extremely hard, if not impossible, to halt once started. Usually it removes the young man's motivation for marriage, destroys their spiritual life, and most often ends up ruining their relationship and they break up. At best, even if they marry, they carry into their wedding bed the unnecessary baggage of guilt.

Don't risk destroying your relationship with guilt by allowing unnecessary body contact to incite your passions and tempt you to disobey God. Relaxed dating in a spirit-controlled environment will produce a wholesome relationship that you can both enjoy without guilt or shame.

If you led a sexually active lifestyle before becoming a Christian and are living with the guilt and shame of your past, I have good news for you. God's Word says, "Therefore, if anyone is in Christ, he is a new creation; old things have passed away; behold, all things have become new" (2 Cor. 5:17).

When Jesus Christ comes into your life, you become a brand new creature — the slate is wiped clean.

From this point on, keep your life pure and holy before God. Don't dwell on the past. Just be grateful you found Him in time. Rejoice that you have a new life and that your body now belongs to Him.

GOD'S WAY TO FIND A MATE

Your loving Heavenly Father is interested in every detail of your life. Most of all, He wants to be vitally involved in the process of choosing the person who will become your life's partner.

Finding a mate for life is serious business, and God has determined several important ground rules that will keep you on track. The Bible calls them "commands" or principles.

Secular educators have probably told you, "There are no blacks and whites in life; everything is in that nice gray zone."

That may sound cool, but such a philosophy leads to confusion and produces intellectual malcontents or psychotics. Why? Because without predetermined principles, making decisions becomes almost impossible. Simple decisions develop into extremely complex issues.

You have two simple choices: black and white. If you violate God's command, that's a black. If you face the temptation and don't give into it, that's a white.

In your lifetime, you will probably have many opportunities to have sex outside of marriage. If, however, you have decided to obey God's Word, you don't have to pray about what you are going to do when a tempting sexual situation arises. You don't have to reorient yourself or restructure your thinking patterns. The Bible says, "Thou shalt not!"

Happy is the individual who calls sin what it is. In this age of semantics, some people try to confuse the issue by putting new labels on old sins.

When a young woman told me she was all confused about the new morality, I replied, "It's not new. It's just plain old immorality. You know, situation ethics — if the situation calls for it, it's fine. If you go back to the Bible and situate yourself, you'll find the situation calls for marriage! There is no alternative."

There is no gray zone in God's Word — only principles and standards. That's why it's so much simpler for Christians to make decisions. That's why Christians can make judgments and have definite, unwavering opinions about social issues.

Some people say, "Well, aren't you Christians an opinionated bunch!"

Yes. In fact, we're very narrow-minded. Why? Because Jesus Christ said it's a "narrow way." It's either Jesus Christ absolutely or not at all. If we are going to follow Jesus, we must obey His commands and the principles laid out for us in God's Word.

Let's look at several biblical principles regarding how a Christian should select a mate for life.

1. Only marry a Christian.

Whenever a young person says to me, "I would like your opinion on my marrying so-and-so," I always respond by asking, "Is so-and-so a Christian?"

If the answer is "I'm not sure" or "I'm praying for him or her," my guess is that the prospective partner is an unbeliever.

When you think about marriage, don't let yourself drift into a gray zone by playing mental footsie with the idea of marrying anyone who isn't a Christian.

If the person you are dating and considering marrying is an unbeliever, that can't possibly be the will of God for you. How can I be so dogmatic? Because God's Word makes it clear:

Do not be unequally yoked together with unbelievers. For what fellowship has righteousness with lawlessness? And what communion has light with darkness? And what accord has Christ with Belial? Or what part has a believer with an unbeliever? And what agreement has the temple of God with idols? For you are the temple of the living God. As God has said: "I will dwell in them And walk among them. I will be their God, And they shall be My people." Therefore "Come out from among them And be separate," says the Lord. "Do not touch what is unclean, And I will receive you. I will be a Father to you, And you shall be My sons and daughters," Says the Lord Almighty (2 Cor. 6:14-18).

What fellowship can light have with darkness? What fellowship can the believer have with an unbeliever?

Occasionally, a sincere Christian young person will say, "Pastor LaHaye, I know you teach that we shouldn't be unequally yoked to unbelievers, but I believe that this time it's different. I'm led of the Holy Spirit."

When I challenge him on it, he responds, "But don't you think I can be led of the Spirit?"

"Yes, I do, but the Bible and the Holy Spirit are never in opposition," I explain. "And God the Holy Spirit will never lead you contrary to what He has written in His Word."

Happy is the individual who decides to go God's way in all things.

As a pastor, I will not, under any circumstances, marry a couple if one is an unbeliever. Why am I so dogmatic about not marrying a couple who will be unequally yoked? Because I've never seen it work out for the good of either partner. In fact, the result is usually a marriage of heartache at best and divorce at worst.

In spite of God's grace and the love He can give through a difficult situation, it never pays to disobey God's Word.

When God's man or God's woman comes your way, you won't have to wonder or question God's will. He or she will come wrapped in so much Christian packaging that there will be no doubt. Then for the rest of your life, you will be able to say, "Every good gift and every perfect gift is from above" (James 1:17).

Don't settle for less than God's good and perfect will for you.

2. Don't confuse sexual attraction for love.

All of us have a physical, magnetic attraction toward certain people. Just as an electromagnet can draw steel to itself, certain types of individuals of the opposite sex attract us more than others. It doesn't really have anything to do with looks, and many people in our society confuse this for love.

Suppose we numbered people — from one to ten — according to this strange, biological magnetic attraction. If you are a five, and you find yourself in close proximity to somebody of your number, your senses come to life. You perceive that someone nearby is on your same wavelength.

After couples are married, the idealists think, *Oh, there's just one person in the world I can be drawn to like that.* Christian psychologist Dr. Henry Brandt has said you could have this magnetic attraction for probably one million people of the opposite sex within your own three-year age bracket in America alone.

If that many of the opposite sex are on your wavelength, they can't all be the one person God has chosen for you. What is it then? Plain old biological, magnetic attraction. While this phenomenon may generate momentary excitement, it also creates many tempting problems.

I once had a secretary who was not only quite beautiful but also very personable and outgoing. Whenever other pastors would come into the office, they would walk in and before they would sit down I'd know exactly what they were going to say: "Good night, LaHaye! How does your wife let you have a secretary like that?"

To tell the truth, I was surprised myself! Actually, I considered her more like a sister, and we worked together well for two years. Why? Because we weren't on the same wavelength.

I'll be honest. That has not been true of all the secretaries I've ever had, or all the women who have ever come into my office.

Where the opposite sex is concerned, I have always maintained a hands-off relationship. The Bible says, "avoid the very appearance of evil," and "make no provision for the flesh." Happy is the man who knows the extent and the inclinations of his flesh and makes no provision for it.

Whenever God brings you together with the right person, he or she will be the same number you are. If you're a ten, then you don't want a six. He or she will also be on the same spiritual wavelength, and you will enjoy unity in Christ.

3. Avoid marrying under pressure.

Over the years, I have counseled with more than one young woman who was distraught over the condition of her marriage.

After pouring out her heart, I couldn't help but ask, "Why in the world did you marry him in the first place?"

"I was unhappy at home. My father was making life miserable for me. This nice guy offered me security, so I married him."

When a young man or woman comes from an unhappy home, he or she may see marriage as a way of escape.

A young man may be tired of his dominating parents and decide that marriage would be a nice way out. A girl who is insecure about her father's love may seek a husband to fulfill the affection she's missing at home.

If you're miserable where you are, a change of circumstance won't make you happy. God is able to give you joy in your present situation or open another door for you. Marriage, however, should never be used as an escape ladder.

Relax and take your time. Enjoy the dating game. If you're not in a hurry, you are more likely to make the right decision. Panic palace is a dreadful place to live, and decisions made under pressure are disastrous. God is not in a hurry.

If you're in love with someone and you think he or she is the person, then commit that person to God and give the relationship time. Let it simmer.

As a pastor, I have an unconditional rule concerning marriages. I will not, under any circumstances, officiate at the wedding unless the two people have gone together for six months — and that's the barest minimum.

Why? Because if you haven't gone with a person with the intention of marriage for six months, you don't really know him or her. I've had this rule long enough to have saved a number of couples from a disastrous experience.

One young lady often stops after church to shake my hand and whisper, "Thank you."

I know why she's so grateful.

She had been dating a young man for only two months and wanted to get married in the church.

I told her, "I can't because you two haven't been going together for six months. And if I don't officiate at the wedding, you can't use the church for the ceremony."

"Okay, we'll wait," she agreed reluctantly.

About the fourth month, she and her fiancée had a big fight and broke up. Within a short time she met and fell in love with Mr. Right. Now they have two children.

Every now and then, she tells me, "I'm so glad I waited for God's man."

4. Test your love by separation.

I'm thoroughly convinced that every serious relationship should be tested by a long period of separation.

> "If you're miserable where you are, a change of circumstance won't make you happy. God is able to give you joy in your present situation or open another door for you. Marriage, however, should never be used as an escape ladder."

Sometimes a young man will go off to school or join the military or take a job that separates him from his girlfriend for several months or a year. When this happens, it gives both a chance to view their relationship more realistically without the constant pressure of dating.

If it is impossible to separate geographically, a couple could decide to refrain from contact for a month or six weeks. During the time of separation, they can assess their true feelings.

When a couple is dating on a regular basis — day after day or week after week — it is difficult to be objective about their relationship. A crucial decision like marriage requires an unbiased, almost analytical process.

During this period of separation — or at some point in your relationship — you need to make sure you are in the center of God's will and that this is the person He wants for you.

5. Learn how to resolve disagreements.

If you and the person you are courting are in constant disunity over minor and major issues, look out!

Some people think arguing is a fact of life between partners — whether they are dating, engaged, or married. Many marriage counselors believe that occasional quarrels between couples are good since they help "clear the air."

A University of Michigan team of doctors discovered, however, that habitual quarrels can impair the health of both partners, increasing the risk of arthritis in wives and ulcers in husbands. These two illnesses seem to arise more frequently in couples who consistently argue, bicker, and quarrel with each other.

A young couple who was experiencing conflict in their relationship, came to me for counseling. "Arguing helps us keep issues out in the open," they told me.

I responded with this question: "How should you — as spirit-filled Christians — view arguing?"

When they couldn't come up with a response, I said, "Any time you raise your voice or get enraged, you're not being controlled by the Holy Spirit; you're being controlled by anger motivated by selfishness."

Then I gave them three suggestions:

A. Back off from any heated discussions.

"Wait until you can let your emotions be controlled by the Spirit," I told them.

"Isn't it more harmful to keep our emotions bottled up inside?" the young man asked.

"No," I replied. "Arguing seldom has a productive outcome."

B. Don't refuse to talk.

Learn to discuss issues without letting your emotions get the best of you. Productive discussion cannot take place in an atmosphere of anger.

The Bible says, "Speak the truth in love."

You don't have to argue and quarrel. You can lovingly discuss as the Holy Spirit leads.

C. Don't let arguing become a habit.

If you work on this area now — before marriage — you can keep arguing from becoming a habitual problem. If, on the other hand, the conflicts in your relationship cannot be resolved without anger, any marriage plans should be put on hold.

Don't marry anyone who cannot control his or her emotions. Unbridled anger can lead to mental and physical abuse.

Anger will put you out of control. When you're angry, you will always make bad decisions — and bad decisions always result in negative consequences.

"It's dangerous for a player to get angry," a football player told me, "because he makes himself vulnerable to serious injury."

This defensive back went on to explain: "Whenever you see us walking back up the field with the wide receiver who's gone down for a pass, what do you think we're saying? We're not inviting him for lunch the next day. We're trying to needle him and make him so mad that he can't make a good, mental decision on the next play." Anger can cause you to make dangerous decisions.

6. Make sure you have the same life goals.

As a couple, you don't have to share everything and you don't have to be exactly alike, but most of your interests should be similar. This is why both partners should be vitally interested in serving Christ.

If you're interested in winning souls and walking the spirit-filled life, don't be satisfied with anyone who isn't. Don't say, "Oh, I'll change him after we're married." Forget it.

When my wife and I were dating at college, I became friendly with her older sister, Barrie, who was also a student.

One day, as I was walking Barrie to her dorm, I said, "I notice you and Bill are seeing a lot of each other. Is your relationship getting serious?"

"Well, I don't know," Barrie answered softly. "You see a few years ago, God spoke to me. And I believe He wants me to be a missionary to the Chinese."

"Oh, that's interesting," I replied — although at the time I didn't even know what a missionary was!

About two weeks later, Bill and I were crossing the campus together, and I said, "Hey, man. You look like you're really intrigued with Barrie. Are you thinking of getting married?"

"Yes, I am," he answered in his usual serious tone.

"When are you going to pop the question?" I asked bluntly. This topic of conversation intrigued me since I had already made up my mind I was going to ask Beverly to marry me.

"Well, I've got another question to ask her first," Bill answered.

"What is it?"

He responded, "When I was in the infantry I was stationed at a base in Texas. My bunkmate was Nate Saint, one of the five missionaries martyred in South America among the Acca Indians. Nate was a unique Christian. I'd never met anyone like him in my life. He was committed to reaching the lost for Christ, and he knew his military training was preparing him to serve the Lord on the mission field. The Holy Spirit used Nate in my life. Since then, God has called me to be a missionary among the Chinese."

I didn't know what to say, so I kept my big mouth shut.

Bill continued, "Before I ask Barrie to marry me, I've got to ask her what God wants to do with her life."

A few days later, I saw Bill floating across the campus, and I knew he had gotten the right answer to both his questions.

Barrie and Bill found not only God's vocation for their lives — they found God's mate for the ministry to which He had called them. Needless to say, they have a storybook marriage.

Whatever your vocation, that's the kind of marriage I hope that you enjoy with the mate God gives you.

7. Determine if your personalities complement each other.

Are you strong where he is weak, and is he strong where you are weak? You'll find that opposites attract each other.

When gregarious George Sanguine arrives at a party, he invigorates the room with his outgoing personality and lively conversation. Everyone notices him — he makes a point of that.

Quiet Susie Melancholy, on the other hand, spends the evening sitting in a corner, looking sweet and demure. She never does anything to draw attention to herself, never says anything wrong, and always laughs at the right time.

All the while, she's admiring George Sanguine and his outgoing, uninhibited manner. Susie thinks, "Oh, what a great guy."

After the party, as George speeds home in his big car — everything he does is big and fast — he talks to himself.

"George, why can't you learn to keep your big mouth shut" he says out loud. "You dominated the whole conversation. Why can't you be like Susie Melancholy. You know, she's so reserved and pretty. She must be smart, too. After all, she laughed at all my jokes. I think I'll give her a call."

As Susie arrives home in her little Honda, she thinks, *What a wonderful guy George is. He's so different from me. If I weren't so shy, maybe he would have shown more interest.*

Suddenly, her phone rings.

"Susie, I noticed you at the party tonight," George begins.

"Oh," she answers, "were you there?"

"How about supper tomorrow night?"

"Well, hold the phone just a moment. I'll check my date book."

After shuffling around for a few moments, she returns to the phone and says, "Well, George, I do have an opening tomorrow night."

They go out for dinner, and after a whirlwind courtship, they marry and — with George in charge — take off on an emotionally supercharged honeymoon.

This marriage is based on need — and that's good because we need each other. Don't marry someone who doesn't need you. You need to be needed. Every living, breathing human being needs someone else.

After the honeymoon, however, George and Susie discover that the subconscious differences that attracted them to each other are accompanied by certain weaknesses.

The day after the honeymoon, they are back in her apartment. They chose to live at her place because his was in a shambles.

The next morning, George wakes up bright-eyed and bushy-tailed — as sanguines usually do. He's in the shower singing away, and Susie is still in a fog. (Melancholies are not early birds.)

When she hears all this racket, Susie realizes she is a wife! Catapulting out of bed, she throws on her perfectly folded robe and begins to make breakfast. George whips through the kitchen just in time for her to present the first burnt offering.

They say their sweet goodbyes, and Susie stumbles back into the bedroom — and the moment of truth.

Her once well-ordered bedroom is a shambles. Susie hadn't noticed it when they went to bed, but he just threw his pants over the chair and his coat on the floor and wadded up his socks next to the bed. And lo and behold, there's a wet towel in the middle of the bed!

In the bathroom, the sink is filled with beard chips and the bath mat is sopping wet. The contents of the medicine cabinet are in a shambles from his hunt for the hair spray — and he didn't even put the cap back on! To make matters worse, he squeezed the toothpaste in the middle of the tube and used her toothbrush on his teeth!

Suddenly, Susie realizes she has an adjustment to make.

It doesn't matter if the man is the melancholy and the woman is the sanguine or vice versa. Whatever the personality types, adjustments have to be made.

If you know beforehand the type of person you are marrying, you will be able to anticipate the differences in your temperaments and lifestyles. If you focus on your partner's strengths and make adjustments for his or her weaknesses, you will have a long, happy marriage.

8. Commit your relationship to the Lord.

If your relationship is spiritually deteriorating, look out! You are walking on dangerous ground — and this happens more often than not. Couples often get more interested in each other than they do in the will of God.

You should be attending church together, praying when you go out on dates, and encouraging one another in your walk with the Lord.

Never get to the place where you're willing to say, "Lord, I want him or her, no matter what!" That's the prayer for disaster.

Happy is the young person who is willing to pray, "Lord, I commit my relationship with him or her to You." Commit your way and the person you love to the Lord.

Always be honest with God. If you love someone, tell God about it. Say, "Lord, I love so-and-so. I want to commit that love to You. If You want it to come to fruition, then You just increase my love. If You don't, then squelch it."

God is the author of love, and He can change your emotions if you submit them to Him. This is where a period of separation can help you assess the situation reasonably.

Then, when you do make a decision, you'll have that peace that passes all understanding.

9. Wait for God's best.

There are probably many people in this world to whom you could be happily married. But there is only one person who is God's best for you.

If you let the Lord make the final decision, you will never have to wonder about your choice of a mate. You will always know that your marriage was ordained by God.

When I first met Steve and his fiancée, their two-year relationship was already stormy.

Although he had been planning to be a history professor, Steve felt that God was calling him to preach the Gospel. He had recently changed his major at college and was studying for the ministry.

His fiancée, an ambitious graduate student, appeared to be the dominant one in their relationship. In fact, she could chew him up and spit him out — and they weren't even married!

I couldn't help but think that the last thing this tender young man needed was a wife with more education and a more forceful personality than he had. His perfectionist temperament was already suffering.

Together, the three of us prayed about their relationship. I suggested they commit it to God and say, "Lord, if You want us to marry, then increase our love; and if You don't want us to marry, cause it to die."

Before I knew it, the engagement was off.

About the same time, a beautiful, outgoing young lady came to me for counseling.

"I've been dating an airline pilot," she told me. "Tom is a Christian, but we don't share the same commitment. I really want to serve the Lord, but he's more drawn to the things of the world."

"Just being equally yoked with a believer is not enough," I told her. "If you want Jesus Christ to use your life, you don't want to saddle yourself with a carnal Christian. You want a Christian who is on your level spiritually — someone motivated to move out for God."

That day she prayed the same prayer as the ministerial student and his fiancée had prayed: "Lord, if You don't want me to marry Tom just take away the feeling I have."

Sure enough, something happened, and the feelings died.

One Sunday morning, as I was seated behind the pulpit getting ready to preach, I noticed Steve, the young ministerial student, about eight rows back. Just at that moment, one of the ushers brought in the lovely young lady who had been dating the airline pilot and seated her right next to him.

When I saw them sitting there together, I looked up and said, "Heavenly Father, did You notice that?"

I'm almost certain I heard God say, "Who do you think arranged it all, anyway?"

My young friend was sharp enough to know he was sitting next to a quality creature. Before she got out the door, he found out where she lived.

Soon they were going together, and every time the church doors were open they were there. They were on the same spiritual level and had many common interests. Her outgoing, vivacious ways complemented his low-key, reserved manner.

When they came to talk to me about setting the wedding date, everything fit. They waited even longer than the six-month period.

I'll never forget their wedding day as long as I live.

About an hour before the wedding, I found her dressed in her gown with the veil flowing out behind and passing out corsages to the wedding party.

I found Steve in the back of the church, pacing up and down, with beads of perspiration on his face.

When everyone was finally in place, she came floating down the aisle. I could tell from the look on his face that there wasn't another person in the church as far as he was concerned.

At the end of the ceremony, I always have the couple bow for prayer at the kneeling bench. When I reached over and put my hands on theirs, I prayed. Then the soloist started to sing "The Lord's Prayer."

When I looked at this brilliant young man with his gifted temperament, I saw tears streaking down his face. She had her eyes closed with a great big smile on her face.

About halfway through the solo, she opened her eyes and saw him wiping tears off his chin. He didn't want to use the handkerchief in the tuxedo, and he didn't have another handkerchief. She quickly sized up the situation, reached down inside her dress for a tissue, and handed it to him.

He took it, wiped his tears, handed it back to her, and she popped it back in her gown. She noticed I had watched the whole thing, so she gave me a wink and one of her vivacious smiles. I knew that couple would make it — and they have. They have joyfully served their Lord together for over 20 years.

Now if there is a moral to that story, it is this: Give God a chance to bring you His best.

Allow me to pray for you:

Heavenly Father, may the young person reading this book not settle for second-rate, but find Your perfect will for life's vocation and a life's partner. We ask this in the name of Jesus Christ, who loved us so much that He literally gave himself for us. Amen.

Alike in Love

When Opposites Attract

A concerned mother phoned me from Arizona. "My daughter and son-in-law are having marital problems," she told me sadly.

"They are currently visiting southern California. If they come to your city, will you see them?"

"Of course," I agreed. "Just have them call to set up a time."

Tuesday evening they arrived at my office, and almost immediately the wife informed me, "Our parents asked us to come to you. That's the only reason we're here."

Now there's a challenge for any marriage counselor.

"Besides, there's no hope for our marriage," the husband added. "Tomorrow we're returning home, and we have an appointment with our attorney on Thursday morning."

"Why are so you convinced it's hopeless?" I inquired.

"We've just returned from a counseling center, where we took a battery of psychological tests," the husband responded. "The counselor concluded that we are hopelessly mismatched."

"What did he suggest?" I asked, knowing such tests are designed by psychologists who don't consider God's Word as the final authority.

"A divorce," the wife stated, dabbing her eyes with a tissue.

The husband looked at me. "What do you think?"

"I'm so glad you asked," I began. "That is the worst advice I've ever heard coming from a so-called Christian counselor."

Shocked, they both stared at me as I continued. "The Bible is very clear on the subject of divorce, is it not?" Neither partner answered.

"The Bible says if you're married, 'seek not to be loosed' — period!" I stated emphatically. "It doesn't take a theologian to figure that out."

"You mean we have to stay married and be miserable the rest of our lives?" the husband whined.

"No, just the first part," I answered with a smile.

I challenge anyone to find two marriage partners who are absolutely compatible in all areas. In fact, no two people on earth are alike. Differences are inevitable when a man and a woman decide to become one in a marriage relationship.

God doesn't expect Christian couples to stay married and be miserable. He wants you to be happy and has given instructions on how to live together in love and harmony.

Back in the first century — when God gave the commands "Husbands, love your wives" and "Wives, submit to your husbands" — most couples were married to partners their parents had selected for them. Young men and women married by faith and stayed married by obeying God.

"But my husband — or wife — is totally opposite from me!" you complain.

Is that grounds for divorce? After all, you chose your mate. Could it be that opposites really do attract one another? If so, then maybe there is a reason for this attraction.

Let me outline the advice I gave the couple who claimed they were "hopelessly mismatched."

How to Adjust to an Opposite Partner

My wife, Bev, and I are total opposites. If there are two ways of doing anything, she will choose one and I will choose the other. It doesn't matter if it's disciplining children or buying food or paying bills or anything else, we just approach life differently.

In spite of our different ways of doing things, Bev and I have a wonderful marriage. After all, it was those very differences that attracted us — as two college sweethearts — to one another. Over the years, we've come to realize that our opposite temperaments have actually worked to our advantage. How? We complement each other. Where she is weak, I am strong — and vice versa. Best of all, it has certainly made life interesting!

Temperament is only one part of our makeup; personality and character comprise the other two parts. Your personality — the way the you project yourself — is actually an outgrowth of your temperament. Character determines who you really are. Sometimes people project a good personality but have a bad character.

Temperament is not personality. What is temperament? The involuntary cause of your actions and reactions that influences approximately 20 to 30 percent of your current behavior. Note the adjective "involuntary." That means it is beyond your control. In fact, your academic interests and vocational abilities often result from the makeup of your temperament.

Although you are born with a certain type of temperament, it can be adjusted and refined by the Holy Spirit and the principles you learn from the Word of God.

By identifying your own — and your mate's — temperament type, you will better understand yourself and your husband or wife.

Identify Your — and Your Mate's —Temperament Type

Each temperament type has strengths and weaknesses. To simplify the four temperament types, we can separate them into two categories: the extroverts and the introverts.

Extroverts are easy to identify: They can't wait to interrupt the person who's talking so they can put in their two cents' worth. You know, "Enough about you; let's talk about me!"

Extroverts usually have a sanguine or a choleric temperament.

Introverts, on the other hand, can outwait anyone. Easy-going and polite, they would never think of barging into a conversation.

The melancholies and the phlegmatics tend to have a more introverted type temperament.

Although Hippocrates is often considered the author of the temperament theory, King Solomon — 500 years before Hippocrates — wrote about four kinds of people in chapter 30 of the Book of Proverbs: melancholies, phlegmatics, sanguines, and cholerics.

THE MELANCHOLY TEMPERAMENT

Proverbs 30:11 describes, in a symbolic way, people who are born with a melancholy temperament: "There is a generation that curses its father, And does not bless its mother."

While this verse does not literally apply to melancholies, it reflects how they generally feel and act toward people. They can find fault with anyone — themselves included.

Thinkers, analyzers, mystics, and musicians usually have a melancholy temperament. These very capable people, however, are often terribly insecure. They don't like anybody or anything. In fact, they sometimes don't even like themselves.

The laid-back temperament of melancholies, however, makes them more gifted in areas that require a great degree of self-discipline and concentration. As a result, they develop their intellect and talents to perfection and are often scholars, artists, concert pianists, and chess players.

Mathematicians almost always have either a melancholy or phlegmatic temperament. You'll find that college professors have a high degree of melancholy because of their analytical capabilities. The sensitive, insecure nature of the melancholic, however, makes him prone to self-introspection and depression.

A melancholic, when giving directions, is not content to say, "Well, you go out here, about three and a half miles until you find another road and you turn to the left." No, he or she will say, "Go three and four-tenth miles, and turn onto the first dirt road across from the large red barn with a black roof."

THE PHLEGMATIC TEMPERAMENT

The 12th verse of Proverbs 30 describes the nice people, the *phlegmatics*. They get along with everybody. "There is a generation that is pure in its own eyes, Yet is not washed from its filthiness." Phlegmatics are super introverts — quiet and diplomatic. Their motto is, "Still waters run deep." These easy-going types seldom get angry or irritated. Nothing ruffles them, and they seem to just float through life. They can come to church for four hours — attend Bible class, worship the Lord during the morning service — and leave without saying much more than "Good morning" and "Goodbye" to a few people.

If you ask him how he's doing, he will answer, "Fine."

It's not that they are against talk; they just don't do it. Maybe it takes too much energy.

I like to be around phlegmatics because they have a great sense of humor. Since they don't like for anyone to be upset, they make jokes to diffuse unpleasant situations.

Some of the best counselors are phlegmatics because they like to listen to people and tend to be very objective. Their practical, utilitarian, and diplomatic approach to life often succeeds in bringing opposing parties together.

	Strengths	*Weaknesses*
Sanguine	Outgoing Warm & Friendly Talkative Enthusiastic Compassionate	Undisciplined Emotionally Unstable Unproductive Egocentric Exaggerates
Melancholy	Gifted Analytical Aesthetic Self Sacrificing Industrious Self-Disciplined	Moody Self-centered Persecution prone Revengeful Touchy Theoretical Unsociable Critical Negative
Choleric	Strong-willed Independent Visionary Practical Productive Decisive Leader	Cold & Unemotional Self-sufficient Impetuous Domineering Unforgiving Sarcastic Angry Cruel
Phlegmatic	Calm Quiet Easygoing Dependable Objective Efficient Organized Practical Humorous	Unmotivated Procrastinator Self-Centered Stingy Self-protective Indecisive Fearful Worrier

These low-key introverts, however, are not perfect. Their biggest problem is motivation — they don't have any. From the time they are born, their inertia level starts running down. As they grow older, they get slower and slower.

If you get them up, keep them moving. If they sit down, they'll relax; and if they relax, they'll fall asleep.

They are masters at procrastination and live by the motto "Always put off until tomorrow." That could be the reason phlegmatics are so indecisive and frequently vacillating between two opinions.

Phlegmatics can spend 30 minutes to an hour every morning getting organized to go to school or work. Then at the end of the day they get organized to go home. They probably do five hours worth of work in an eight-hour day. Phlegmatics love details and precision, which makes them great engineers and math teachers. In fact, these compulsive neat-nicks will organize anything that's not nailed down.

Phlegmatics are also very conservative. Unfortunately, they conserve everything — even their love. Underneath their nice, gentle spirit, they can be very selfish, self-protecting individuals. They don't like to give too much of their love — or themselves — because they might be hurt.

As natural born worriers they are plagued by fear, worry, and anxiety. This could be why they are prone to be frugal and stingy with money. They have to learn to be generous.

On the positive side, phlegmatics often exhibit more Christ-like behavior before they become Christians than the rest of us do afterward. They are wonderful people if they can get their emotions under control.

The Sanguine Temperament

The two extrovert temperaments are the *sanguine* (the super extrovert) and the *choleric* (the managerial type).

Verse 13 of Proverbs 30 describes this third temperament: the *sanguine*. "There is a generation — oh, how lofty are their eyes! And their eyelids are lifted up."

Sanguines are constantly looking around. Why? Because their focus is always, "Where is my audience?"

These attention-seeking, fast-talking, super-extroverts have charisma to burn. With a tendency to stretch the truth, sanguines like to exaggerate to make a point or add punch to the punch line.

If you have ever bought a used car, the salesman was probably a sanguine. Who else could sell a pile of junk and call it a car? These wonderful, friendly types relate well to everyone they meet and are great at public relations.

If you want someone to communicate with — actually you'll mostly just listen — get a sanguine. You may have to tell him *what* to communicate, but he can communicate better than anyone I know. They have so much charm, you want to do whatever they say even though you don't want to do it. That's the effect they have on people.

Sanguines, on the other hand, are generally not academically inclined; they focus on people and find it difficult to concentrate for long periods of time. Sanguines and cholerics usually don't excel at math or spelling, but they do well in history and political science.

Like all the temperament types, sanguines have some serious weaknesses. Although they have tremendous charisma and ability, they lack self-discipline and have a hard time channeling their efforts in the right direction.

Oddly enough, sanguines are very compassionate. If you want a doctor with a good bedside manner, always go to Dr. Sanguine. When he comes into the hospital room where you are lying pale as a ghost and on the verge of death, his eyes are full of concern. Dr. Sanguine walks over, takes your hand, and rubs it.

Your heart begins to palpitate, blood comes back into your face, and you appear to be alive. Then out the door he goes! He forgets to look at your chart because sanguines are careless about details . . . and you die. Don't feel bad — all his patients die happy.

The Choleric Temperament

Verse 14 of Proverbs 30 describes the *choleric* person: "There is a generation whose teeth are like swords, And whose fangs are like knives, To devour the poor from off the earth, And the needy from among men."

This character is tough and determined — the master sergeant type. He wants to be in charge of every situation. When he sets his jaw to do something, nothing can dissuade him.

This dominating, dictator-type personality knows how to order people around and guide them through life. Saddam Hussein is probably a choleric. This type of person thrives on opposition. If you say, "You can't do that!" they say, "Watch me!"

The modus operandi of the choleric is usually "the end justifies the means." They do whatever they think is expedient. If their actions are questioned, they simply try to justify themselves. Cholerics are visionaries. They are constantly making goals and dreaming dreams, yet they sometimes have trouble putting their plans into action.

Not a perfectionist by nature, the extrovert choleric does tend to be well-organized, practical, and utilitarian. Since they are also very productive, they are prone to become workaholics. A choleric husband will tell his wife, "I am away so much because I work long and hard so I can make things better for you and the kids." The truth is they love to work. Cholerics are also very decisive. They don't vacillate between two decisions. When they make up their mind, they do it. They're what business calls SNL's — strong, natural leaders.

Along with all these good traits come some serious weaknesses. One is lack of emotion. They're not affectionate people and can actually be cold and indifferent.

This attitude reflects their cut and dry approach to life — a quality that also makes cholerics very self-sufficient. "I can do very well by myself, thank you," is their attitude. Since they don't like to beat around the bush, they can quickly cut a person down to size with their sarcastic tongue.

Further on the down side, they are impetuous, domineering, and unforgiving. You get one strike in their ball game and, "That's it! I trusted you 35 years ago, and you failed me! Don't think I have forgotten!"

> "Although you are born with a certain type of temperament, it can be adjusted and refined by the Holy Spirit and the principles you learn from the Word of God."

Face the Fact That Opposites Attract

Two people of the same temperament type almost never get married. Why? Because like temperaments repel, they don't attract.

Two sanguines would never get married. They might date for a while, but their relationship would be so emotionally supercharged it wouldn't last. Besides, one of them would have to stop talking long enough to listen — and that would never happen. Eventually, they would get bored because, as Shakespeare said to the sanguine, "All the world's a stage." Who wants to be a performer without an audience? Both would be vying for center stage, and that never works.

Two cholerics would rarely marry. In fact, they would rarely go out together unless someone else arranged a blind date. Even then they would get into a fight before they got to the car. Where are we going? Who's going to drive? Who's going to pay? They would be home in an hour.

Two phlegmatics might date. They'd go together, go together, and go together, but they'd both die of old age before one got up enough steam to ask the other one to marry.

Two melancholies could date for a while since their temperament spectrum has a broad range. In a sadistic mood, they might even decide to marry each other — but it's not very likely.

Why do opposites attract each other? Why wouldn't two cholerics get together? Why wouldn't two phlegmatics marry? Wouldn't it be simpler if you had two organized people living together? No. Your marriage needs the strengths of the other temperament to make it work.

After years of struggling to manage our family finances, I finally admitted: I'm a terrible bookkeeper. When balancing the family checkbook my motto was: Who cares as long as it's close?

I used to keep a pair of bank accounts. For about four months, I would write checks on one account until all the checks came in on the other account. Then I would use the second account until the first one settled and I had some idea of how much money I had left. Over the course of a year it never cost me more than $10 or $12! Besides, one account was always within four months of being accurate.

One day as Bev and I were walking through the bank, the banker — who was a friend of ours — called my wife over and said, "Mrs. LaHaye, would it be possible to get your husband to turn the bookkeeping over to you?"

That night, we had a "honey" talk, and I agreed that she should take over keeping the checking account balanced.

About two months later I found her sitting at the dining room table worriedly shifting through a pile of checks. After about three hours, I finally asked, "Honey, what are you doing?"

Without glancing up, she said, "I'm looking for ten cents."

Ten cents? "Here, I'll give you ten cents!" I shouted in amazement. "Stop wasting your time!

"No," she replied emphatically. "I can't quit until I find it!"

Since I understand her temperament, I didn't argue. I knew that's the way she's wired. She finally found the ten missing pennies.

We have different temperaments. Since we are aware of our different strengths and weaknesses, I don't try to make her like me, and she accepts me for what I am. We respect our differences.

Once you realize, "That's the way he, or she, is," back off. Stop trying to change your mate. That's how God created him or her. The sooner you accept your differences, the better your marriage will be.

Admit to Yourself, "I'm Not Perfect"

We are all subconsciously attracted to someone who is strong where we are weak. You're not attracted to a person who has the same weaknesses as yours. Why? Because you hate your own weaknesses. That's natural.

When you see someone who is strong where you are weak, you become infatuated. You enjoy spending time with that person. Infatuation leads to admiration, and admiration leads to association. Association can lead to love and, hopefully, love leads to marriage.

Since temperament spontaneously influences almost everything we do, it not only affects where our strengths lie but determines our weaknesses. The way a person drives a car depends on his temperament.

Cholerics drive in and out of lanes and take every shortcut in an effort to save a minute going to church or to work.

Sanguines are often dangerous drivers because they are so people-oriented. If you sit in the front, it's okay. If you sit in the back, he'll be turning around to talk to you — and that can be hazardous to your health.

Melancholies drive exactly right. I mean, they rarely get tickets, they always drive one mile under the speed limit — never over the speed limit, and everything is perfect.

Phlegmatics drive about 15 miles under the speed limit and come to a complete stop before entering the on-ramp of the freeway, creating a long line of traffic behind them. Phlegmatics never get into accidents; they cause them.

Temperament also determines our eating habits. Sanguines are often overweight for two reasons: They have no self-discipline, and they eat too fast. Since sanguines do everything fast, they gulp down their meals in ten minutes. They gain weight because it takes 20 minutes for food to enter your stomach and shut off your hunger pangs. By that time, a sanguine has had two meals! Then he feels over-stuffed and has to swallow a roll of Tums.

The choleric, who must always be busy doing something, gains weight because he likes the oral satisfaction of chewing.

The melancholic, however, never eats anything without analyzing the fine print to decode the calorie content, the nutritional value, and the presence of any additives that may have an adverse chemical effect on the environment — particularly his.

The phlegmatics almost never get fat. Why? They eat very slowly and often stop before they finish the entire meal. A phlegmatic child should never be forced to clean his plate. Let him eat what he wants at meals, but avoid snacks in between.

Our emotional makeup and the way we react to people and situations comes from our temperament.

When the sanguine gets mad, he blows up quickly, rakes you over the coals, and then forgets all about it. He never carries a grudge and never gets ulcers — he just gives them to everybody else.

The choleric is also quick to get angry, but he has a hard time letting go of it. He or she tends to harbor resentment, and by the time the choleric is 48 years old — unless he allows the Holy Spirit to change him — he'll either be a Rolaids addict or on his way to the grave.

By now, you have probably found yourself in one of these temperaments — or you may have identified traits from one or more. Actually, most people have a primary temperament and a secondary temperament. I have never met a 100 percent sanguine person. If he existed, he could sell the earth! Nor have I encountered an individual who is 100 percent choleric (he would probably run the earth).

Imagine a man who has a primary temperament that is 60 percent sanguine and a secondary temperament of 40 percent choleric. Look out! This "san-clor" would be a super-extroverted leader.

How about a "san-mel" — a sanguine/melancholic? She would be a highly emotional person prone to cry at telephone numbers and birds that fly overhead.

A "san-phleg" — a sanguine/phlegmatic — would be a self-indulgent, happy floater who would sink into bankruptcy by the time he was 40 years of age. A nice person, but not very productive.

Suppose someone's primary temperament is 60 percent choleric and 40 percent sanguine. That would create a "clor-san" — an extroverted, highly energetic leader and producer.

The two worst workaholics are the cholerics and the melancholic. A 60-40 "clor-mel" would always be crusading for some cause or trying to change something and make it better.

The "clor-phleg" — a 60-40 choleric phlegmatic — would make a great administrator. Gentle and diplomatic because of the phlegmatic, he would be forceful enough to supervise people without dominating them.

A 60-40 "mel-san" would make a great teacher because the sanguine has the ability to say it, and the melancholy has something to say. If we turned it around, however, we might get a teacher who talks too much about nothing.

The "mel-clor" person makes a gifted medical doctor. In fact, I am not sure a doctor could get through medical school without some melancholy. This part of his temperament provides him with a high IQ and the ability to look at words and remember them.

A person who is 60 percent phlegmatic and 40 percent sanguine makes for a very congenial, people-oriented individual who is often medical or service oriented.

The "phleg-clor" has great leadership potential and makes a good administrator.

The "phleg-mel" creates a superb scholar who wouldn't be an irritator.

As you find yourself and your mate in one or more of these categories, the realization has probably dawned that you have weaknesses, too. After all, your mate has pointed them out many times! Cut yourself a break and admit, "I'm not perfect, either." It will do wonders for your own self-esteem and set you free from unrealistic expectations.

ACCEPT YOUR PARTNER'S TEMPERAMENT

Don't conflict with your partner's temperament. If your partner is a sanguine, expect him or her to be loud, self-centered, and seemingly arrogant. Of course, this kind of behavior varies by degrees, but a sanguine will never be a phlegmatic.

Your mate cannot change his in-born temperament. That means the ball is in your court. It's up to you to understand why your mate acts that way and work with it. You married him or her. Something about his temperament type must have appealed to you in the beginning. Now you need to accept it by giving thanks to God.

A dear friend of ours — a well-known author whose name you would recognize — told us an amusing story about her marriage. A lovely sanguine, this lady is outgoing, bubbly, and writes Christian books. Her husband is just the opposite; he is a melancholy accountant and banker.

One day she shared with me how my little book, *Spirit Controlled Temperament*, was used by God in their lives.

Nothing irritated her more than the way her husband always checked up on her. She described how they would crawl into bed at night, and he'd put his big, brawny arm under her neck. As she snuggled next to him, she would find herself responding to his rather amorous mood. Then all of a sudden, he'd stop and call her by name, and say, "Did you lock the back door?"

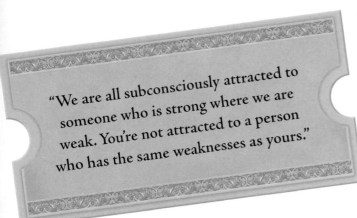

"We are all subconsciously attracted to someone who is strong where we are weak. You're not attracted to a person who has the same weaknesses as yours."

That question didn't bother her because locking the door was her responsibility. She'd reply, "Yes, I did."

Suddenly, he would jerk his arm out from under her neck, leap out of bed, run through the dining room into the kitchen, and check the back door. By then, she was fuming! What a put-down! His actions indicated he didn't trust her. By the time he came back to bed, you can be sure he was crawling in with an iceberg.

The next night, they repeated the same charade. She would start to respond to his mood, and all of a sudden he'd say, "Honey, did you lock the back door?" Sure enough, he'd race and check it.

As she read my book on the different temperament types, she realized her husband was a melancholy. As an accountant, he focused on precision in everything he did. It takes a melancholy to be a successful accountant. In fact, I've never met a sanguine accountant who made any money. He could sell the service for someone else, but he would never have the self-discipline to sit for hours checking and rechecking numbers on balance sheets.

That night she walked through the dining room where her husband was working on a client's tax return. She watched as he went down the 1040 form, adding up a column of figures. Then he wrote down his answer, turned it over and went down the same column and added them again, wrote it down and turned it over. Then he started at the bottom, went up, wrote it down, turned it over, and came down again — four times.

Her husband didn't know she was watching, but as he turned the first piece of paper over, he smiled. Then the second one. His smile got bigger and bigger and bigger as all four figures were the same. Since they all agreed, he wrote the final number at the bottom of the form.

Then she suddenly realized! "He doesn't just check up on me, he checks up on himself!"

A perfectionist doesn't only expect perfection from his mate. He is as critical of himself as he is of you.

That night she was ready for him. He put his arm under her neck, and she responded to him. Then at the crucial moment, he asked, "Did you lock the back door?" She said, "Yes, I did, honey, but if you want to check it, go ahead." Sure enough, he did.

She was different that night when he came back to bed because she understood his temperament. The temperament theory helps you understand your partner so you can work with him or her to create harmony in your relationship.

Focus on Your Mate's Strengths

When you face the fact that you are not perfect, you can accept the fact that your partner isn't perfect, either. Your partner has weaknesses. When opposite temperament types marry, their strengths and weaknesses are also opposite. A partner who is strong in one area can't understand why his or her mate is so weak in that area. Problems escalate when the stronger partner becomes critical of the weaker mate's inability to rise to the expected level of competency in that area.

There's no nakedness like psychological nakedness. When you open your total self to your mate, your strengths — as well as your weaknesses — are exposed. In the early years of marriage, every week that passes uncovers another weakness. We assume that our mate is going to see all those weaknesses, overlook them, and love us anyway. After all, doesn't the Bible say, "Love covers a multitude of sins." *Surely, he or she will ignore my little imperfections and concentrate on my gifts and talents.*

Okay, so you married a sinful, fallen member of the human race — join the club. All of us "have sinned and come short of the glory of God" (Rom. 3:23).

Some spouses make matters worse by mulling over in their minds, *What if? What if?* No matter whom you marry, you could ask, "What if?" Nothing will destroy love like concentrating on your partner's imperfections and comparing her or him to Mr. or Ms. Perfect next door.

Instead of focusing on the weaknesses of your partner, accept them, make permission for them, and concentrate on your partner's strengths. Isn't that what caused you to fall in love in the first place?

The Bible instructs us to concentrate on the good things about one another: "Finally, brethren, whatever things are true, whatever things are noble, whatever things are just, whatever things are pure, whatever things are lovely, whatever things are of good report, if there is any virtue and if there is anything praiseworthy — meditate on these things" (Phil. 4:8).

The eight characteristics cited in this verse are all positive.

When a person tells me, "I married on a wave of love, and now the love is gone," I make this suggestion: "You can create love by concentrating on your partner's strengths and refusing to dwell on his or her weaknesses."

An engineer from our church was married to an outgoing, bubbly, choleric-sanguine who was all energy. Respected among the church women, she exhibited all the qualities a pastor looks for in a godly leader. She had a way of organizing events and getting the other women to go along with anything she suggested. I had great expectations for her.

I was surprised one day when her husband — a quiet, sober-minded, statistician engineer — came to me for counseling. I could tell he was uptight. When I asked him why he had come, he started spilling out his feelings about his wife. As he talked, my image of her became contaminated by the ugly picture he was painting. Depressed and disillusioned, I prayed silently, "Lord, what should I say to this fellow?"

Finally, I looked him in the eye and said, "You know it's really a shame you married such a lousy woman."

His back stiffened, and he said, "Well, now, my wife isn't that bad."

"Can you tell me anything good about her?" I asked.

He thought for a couple of minutes and came up with a positive characteristic.

"Anything else?"

"Yes . . ." he responded with another good trait.

"Anything else?"

As he started to mention a third attribute, a smile crossed his face. "LaHaye, I know what you're doing."

Sure, I was trying to take his magnifying glass of criticism off his wife's weaknesses and put it back where it was when he fell in love with her . . . focused on her strengths.

Everyone has strengths and weaknesses. Your feelings of love or disdain toward your mate will be in direct proportion to the amount of time you focus your thoughts and attention on the negatives. Some people are born critics — especially those with a melancholy temperament. That's why I told my engineer friend, "Throw away your magnifying glass and concentrate on the praiseworthy aspects of your wife's character."

The same thing is true about your partner. Concentrate on your partner's strengths, and never, never permit yourself to indulge in dwelling on their weaknesses. Certain flaws in your mate's character cannot be overlooked and need to be addressed. When your partner has a weakness that drives you crazy and causes real problems in your marriage, don't let it eat away at you. I suggest you talk about the problem, and openly and lovingly confront your mate. If nothing changes and you come to an impasse, let it go for awhile. Once you've pressed the issue long enough, don't

keep bringing it up. If you constantly nag your mate, you will destroy your relationship and sabotage any meaningful discussions about other issues.

"What else can I do?" you ask. "It still bothers me."

Face the fact that he or she may be unwilling — or unable — to change at this stage of his or her life. There is nothing more you can do except talk to your Heavenly Father about the problem. Lay your burden down, and cast all your cares on Him. Commit the situation to the Lord, and give Him time to work it out.

Begin to pray consistently for the strengthening of your partner's weakness. Pray with deep humility, realizing that you are not perfect either. As you pray, the Holy Spirit may begin to reveal areas in your own life that need changing.

Avoid criticizing your mate mentally or verbally. That does nothing positive. Praying does. You have probably heard the expression, "Prayer changes things" — and it does. It often changes the heart of the one who does the praying. At the same time, God will hear and begin to bring answers when you pray. Give God time to work.

BE QUICK TO APOLOGIZE

Men, don't be like the west Texan who moved to California.

Late one Sunday night, his wife called me and said, "Can you come right over?"

They had just had a huge argument, and as I was trying to piece the facts together, she sobbed, "In the 24 years we've been married, he has never apologized to me."

I turned to him and asked, "Is that true?"

"Yep!" he replied, looking me in the eye.

"How come? Have you never done anything wrong?"

"Oh, yeah, I've done things wrong."

"Well, how come you never apologize?"

"Well, I don't think it's very manly."

This six foot four weight lifter — with muscles bulging out all over his body — is afraid to apologize to his 110 pound wife because it isn't manly.

I talked to him for a while, trying to get to the source of the problem.

Abruptly, he finally blurted out, "My pa never apologized to my mother in 30 years of marriage!"

"Just because your father made 30 years of mistakes, there's no reason for you to continue making them. Do you know what the Bible has to say about this?" I asked him.

"No," he mumbled.

"It says, 'Confess your faults one to another.' Do you know what happens when you confess? God reaches down into your wife's heart and pulls out what could become a root of bitterness." The more we talked, the more he realized the damage that results when one partner is too proud to ask forgiveness.

You can do something dreadful, but if you sincerely apologize — and your partner decides to forgive you — the Holy Spirit can keep that incident from being a tragedy.

Verbalize Your Love

I received a sad letter from a wife whose 42-year-old husband was going through a time of uncertainty in his career and carnality in his spiritual life.

Suddenly, during one of their arguments, she blurted out: "You know, I don't think I love you anymore."

Her statement may have reflected the honest emotion she had at the moment, but she should have kept it to herself. Transitory feelings can be very deceitful.

Her husband started thinking about what she had said and decided he didn't love her either.

"Now we are living apart," she wrote. "We've only been separated for four weeks, and I realize what a fool I was. I really do love him."

My question to her would be, "Why did you let four weeks pass without apologizing and telling him how you really feel?" When we let too much time lapse between our expressions of love, negative emotions will rush in and fill the gap.

Over the years I have noticed that two temperament types have difficulty expressing their love: melancholies and cholerics.

Since cholerics are perfectionists — and almost impossible to please — they seldom feel that anyone is worthy of their love.

Usually a strong leader, the choleric often withholds affection or praise as a means of motivation — at least that's the way the choleric sees it. In an effort to challenge his or her mate — or kids, employees, students — the choleric sets high standards and waits for them to be met before bestowing love or commendation. As a result, those who live and work with the choleric constantly crave his or her approval. In fact, the more choleric you are, the more other people desire your approval. Once you realize this, you need to look for opportunities to bestow that pat on the back or word of encouragement — and don't be afraid to say, "I love you" often and repeatedly to your family.

Don't expect everybody to perform as perfectly or efficiently as you do. Give others room to make mistakes — especially your mate and your children.

The melancholy person also has difficulty expressing love and affection. Why? Because he or she has a long checklist of 21 standards of perfection. If you're only a 20, the melancholy can't say, "I love you" today, because you didn't measure up. Instead, he thinks, *I'm sorry, but you didn't make the grade. Try again tomorrow.*

If you are a melancholy, you also set very high standards for yourself. That's why you're usually grumpy. Lighten up! Learn to enjoy life and other people. Give your mate a hug and say, "I love you," whether you feel like it or not. As you verbally express your love and physically show it, true affection will naturally grow in your heart.

We serve a God of love. He loves us and expects us to love one another. You may say, "She knows I love her. I don't have to tell her. I show it by the things I do for her."

Showing is good. In fact, "God so loved the world that He gave His only begotten Son." God showed His love for us by giving His most precious gift. Jesus also showed His love for us by willingly dying for our sins.

In addition to His acts of love, Jesus repeatedly expressed His love for His disciples — and for us — in words. "A new commandment I give to you, that you love one another; as I have loved you, that you also love one another" (John 13:34). "He who has My commandments and keeps them, it is he who loves Me. And he who loves Me will be loved by My Father, and I will love him and manifest Myself to him" (John 14:21).

When we withhold love from our mate, we disobey the commands of Jesus.

Many years ago I appeared as a guest on the "Phil Donahue Show" to discuss my best-selling book, *The Act of Marriage.* At the end of the program — with 30 seconds left — Phil asked: "Dr. LaHaye, can you give me — in one word — the most destructive force in marriage? What causes marriages to break down most of the time?"

"One word? Yes, I can," I replied. "Selfishness."

It doesn't matter what temperament you or your mate are. If one of you is selfish in your relationship, you will destroy that relationship.

The Bible says, "Let each of you look out not only for his own interests, but also for the interests of others" (Phil. 2:4). Look out for whom? Others. An unselfish person is others-conscious.

In a marriage relationship, instead of looking at what the other person is doing to you — or has done to you — maybe you need to consider what you have done to your partner. Maybe you need to decide, *I'm going to treat my mate unselfishly.* Why? Unselfishness is love.

The 13th chapter of 1 Corinthians lists nine characteristics of love: Love is courteous, love is kind, love is generous, humble, patient, love has good temper, love is sincere, love is guileless, and love is unselfish.

Husbands, if you want to be loved by your mate, be kind to her. All a woman really wants is kindness. If you give her love and kindness, you will never have to worry about her being unfaithful.

"A new commandment I give to you, that you love one another; as I have loved you, that you also love one another" (John 13:34).

God has given human beings the ability to transmit thoughts into another person's head by the vehicle of words. It's called communication. Husbands, your wife needs to hear you say, "I love you." In fact, God commands husbands to love their wives. How? "Husbands, love your wives, just as Christ also loved the church and gave Himself for her" (Eph. 5:25). God gave His "Word" to reassure us. He doesn't want us to be constantly wondering, "Does God love me?" Throughout Scripture, God communicates His love for you and me through words.

> *"Avoid criticizing your mate mentally or verbally. That does nothing positive. Praying does. You have probably heard the expression, 'Prayer changes things' — and it does. It often changes the heart of the one who does the praying."*

As a husband, you need to communicate your love verbally. Why? To reassure your wife, to comfort her, and make her feel secure in your relationship. A wife — after five to ten years of marriage — will reflect her husband's treatment.

If your wife shows signs of being depressed, apprehensive, or on the verge of a neurotic condition, she may need a good dose of your unconditional love and approval. Husband, if you have used your tongue like a whiplash and cut her down and chopped her up into little pieces, you need to ask her forgiveness, tell her you love her, and change your ways.

"Love her, love her, love her, love her." Four times in Ephesians 5, this command is repeated. "Husband, love your wife!" Love her with your voice.

Try it; you'll be amazed at the result.

Be Thankful for Your Mate

The Bible says, "In everything give thanks; for this is the will of God in Christ Jesus for you" (1 Thess. 5:18). Do you know the best way to perpetuate love in your marriage? Give thanks for your partner every day.

In my years of marriage counseling, very few wives have told me, "I don't love my husband anymore." A women's love is elastic — it stretches — but a man's love is rather short and brittle.

One day, as I was having lunch with a friend, he began telling me that his love for his wife was gone. "I have no feelings for her," he said frankly. "In fact, we haven't shared the same bedroom for three months."

I don't know how it is where you live, but in California that's a sure sign all is not well.

After he finished talking, I looked at him and asked, "How would you like to fall madly in love with your wife in three weeks' time?"

"Is it possible?" he asked suspiciously.

"Yes, sir."

"But we've been having problems for a long time, and it's just getting worse."

"I guarantee that if you do what I tell you to do, you will fall in love with her in three weeks." At that point, I reached into my pocket where I usually carry index cards. Taking one out, I said, "You've criticized your wife for 30 minutes, now tell me something good about her."

He thought for ten minutes and came up with one positive point, and then another and then another. As he talked, I wrote down ten. Then I gave him the card and said, "I want you to thank God for each of those ten things twice each day — every morning when you have your devotional time and then every evening."

He just stared at me.

"You said it takes 35 minutes to get from your office to your house," I continued. "While you're driving, I want you to pull out that card and thank God for those ten good things about your wife before you arrive home. In three weeks, you'll fall madly in love with her."

Ten days later, after the Sunday night church service, my friend and his wife came waltzing down the side aisle as everyone else was filing out. As they stood in front of me, he put his arm up on her shoulder, and she snuggled up next to him.

We exchanged a few pleasantries, and then they turned to leave. As she started out a little ahead of him, he turned around toward me and — in a stage whisper that could be heard out on the sidewalk — said, "Hey, we're back in the same bedroom!"

Indeed!

A couple of weeks later, I was going through the San Diego Airport when I had to call his office on business. When we finished our discussion, I asked, "By the way, how are things at home?"

He just about melted into the phone as he said, "Oh, it's super! Better than it's ever been before."

Suddenly, I realized that it had been three weeks to the day since we had first made the list. "Tell me," I said, "Do you have those ten things memorized?"

He surprised me by saying, "Oh, I had those memorized the third day. But you know what I did, I turned that card over and wrote 15 other things I like about her."

If ten won't do it, then you husbands may want to try 25.

This three-week guarantee has worked for many couples, but it does take some discipline. Not only must you thank God twice a day for the ten good things, you must also refuse to think anything negative about your partner. Once you train your mind to ignore the negatives, they become insignificant and fade away in light of the positive areas on which you are focusing.

Later, my friend's wife told me that when he came home the first two or three evenings, she couldn't figure out what was wrong. He was in such a good mood — and being so sweet — that she tried to smell his breath to see if he had been drinking.

This was quite a change from his previous behavior. As a choleric melancholy, his perfectionism had made him very critical of everything his wife did. In fact, she told me she had dreaded hearing his car pull into the driveway. "Oh, boy, this is where I get it. I wonder what I've done wrong today?" she would say.

About the fourth night, she was actually looking forward to seeing him. His attitude had carried over and changed her, too. Love is infectious. So are criticism, hate, bitterness, and animosity.

Make sure that you thank God for your partner every day, and then expect God to bring about change in both of you.

Allow the Holy Spirit to Strengthen Your Weaknesses

Over the years, I have performed more than 350 weddings. Every couple I have married has one objective in common: Happiness. They think marriage is going to produce happiness. I don't try to tell them any different; they'll find that out soon enough.

If marriage doesn't guarantee happiness, what does? The Bible reveals the secret of happiness: "Blessed are they whose ways are blameless, who walk according to the law of the Lord" (Ps. 119:1).

What is the converse of that principle? Miserable are they who don't follow the laws of God.

Jesus said, "Happy" or "Blessed are they that hear the Word of God" and what? "Keep it." It's not enough to hear it — you have to keep it.

In John 13:17, Jesus said, "If you know these things" — the principles of God — "blessed are you if you do them."

You not only have to know the principles of God, you have to do them. The good news is: We don't have to do it on our own. When you invited Jesus Christ into your life, His Holy Spirit came to dwell within you. He is your helper. You have His supernatural power within you to help you live the Spirit-filled life. When a natural human being is indwelt by a supernatural power, that person ought to be different. Right?

In what way should you be different? Has the indwelling Holy Spirit made you better looking since you were saved? Did you get any smarter or more talented? I doubt it.

Your natural strengths may have been enhanced, but the Holy Spirit doesn't create any new physical, mental, or ability changes. So where does the change take place? It takes place in our emotions. The Holy Spirit helps us control our emotions. Look at the nine fruits of the Spirit. They all relate to areas of emotions that we — in the natural — are unable to control on a consistent basis. These fruit bring nine strengths into our life: "Love, joy, peace, longsuffering, kindness, goodness, faithfulness, gentleness, and self-control" (Gal. 5:22-23).

Every person is a composite of strengths on the one hand, and weaknesses on the other. If you desire to be strong in the Lord and in the power of His might, then seek to overcome your weaknesses by receiving the infilling of the Holy Spirit.

Christian psychologist Dr. Henry Brandt defines a mature person: "A mature person is not a perfect person, but he is sufficiently objective about himself to know both his strengths and his weaknesses, and has a planned program for overcoming his weaknesses."

If you are mature, you need a planned program for overcoming your weaknesses. Fortunately, there is not a weakness in your life that cannot be fortified by one of the strengths of the Spirit-filled life. Once you identify your temperament type, you can ask the Spirit of God to strengthen your weaknesses and bring your strengths under His control.

When you are filled with the Holy Spirit, you don't cease being your native temperament. You are what you are, and you will be that way for life. The Holy Spirit, however, acts as your helper to keep you from being driven or dominated by your weaknesses.

Let's look at several Bible characters whose temperaments were refined by the Holy Spirit.

Moses, the melancholy, was a brooder and a thinker. After all, anyone who could sulk for 40 years on the backside of the desert must have surely battled with bouts of depression. How, then, can a man at 80 years of age become one of the greatest leaders the world has ever known? He was transformed by the power of the Holy Spirit.

Moses — like all men — was not perfect. He still indulged in bitterness and hostility and died before his time because he never surrendered his angry disposition to God.

Moses was the only man who broke all Ten Commandments at the same time. In a fit of rage, he threw them down — and we've been using a second-hand set of Ten Commandments ever since!

Abraham appears to have been a phlegmatic since, in his early years, he was afraid of everything. God, however, changed him from a fear-prone wimp to a great man of faith.

The apostle Peter's behavior as revealed in the four gospels exposes an outgoing, gregarious extrovert — a definite sanguine temperament. Although he had leadership potential, his lack of discipline and self-control kept getting him into trouble.

After Peter was filled with the Holy Spirit he became a controlled extrovert. Instead of blurting out the first words that came to his mind, he began to think and engage his brain with his tongue.

The words Peter spoke and wrote — as recorded in the New Testament — were meaningful, uplifting, and helpful. His Spirit-controlled sanguine temperament enabled him to become a positive and effectual leader.

Saul's choleric temperament made him a raving religious zealot who — like a fiery dragon — was "breathing out threatenings and slaughter" as he tortured and imprisoned every man, woman, or child who refused to deny Christ. After he was transformed by the Holy Spirit, the apostle Paul became a compassionate, tenderhearted leader in the early church.

God can change you, but He doesn't change your temperament or other personal characteristics. What does He change? Your weaknesses.

As you submit your will to the ministry of the Spirit of God, you will be gradually fortified with love, joy, peace, patience, kindness, goodness, faithfulness, gentleness, and self-control. The fruit of the Spirit will become the strength of your temperament — much to your mate's delight!

DECIDE TO WALK IN THE SPIRIT

I'd like to ask you a couple of personal questions. Have you been walking in the Spirit in your home during the past week? How have you treated your partner and your children?

God's Word tells us: "If we live in the Spirit, let us also walk in the Spirit" (Gal. 5:25). That's the key to marital happiness even if you and your mate are total opposites.

My wife and I try to walk in the Spirit most of the time, but it's not always easy. Since we are nearly totally opposite in temperament, we have different tastes in colors, in the way we work, and in our personal habits.

Bev is an early riser, and I'm a late night person. By 8:30 in the evening, she can barely hold her eyes open. I've learned not to ask her to do anything after 8:00 that requires a degree of mental alertness. In the morning, however, she's up, singing and happy. And me? I don't even know who I am.

I'm a very goal-oriented person. My motto is: "From production to perfection." If you're going to do something, let's get moving and do it.

Not Bev. She wants to get every detail lined up beforehand with all her ducks in a row. "From perfection to production" — that's her style.

Consequently, Bev and I have difficulty making decisions. If we both did not continually strive to live Holy Spirit-controlled lives, we probably wouldn't be married today. To God goes all the glory for the long, wonderful marriage we have enjoyed.

About three years into our marriage, when I was a church pastor — and Bev a pastor's wife — we were not happily married. If we had been asked to rate our marriage from zero to 100, I would have scored it about 20. Bev was more generous — about 24. Today, we would put it somewhere between 100 and 110!

What happened to us? God the Holy Spirit changed us.

As a minister of the gospel, I had always depended on the Holy Spirit to preach and to bring people to Christ. Even in marriage, Bev and I sought the Holy Spirit's wisdom in the big decisions of life. When it came to our marriage, however, I knew nothing about walking in the control of the Holy Spirit at home. Yet, that's where "the rubber meets the road" in the Spirit-controlled life.

The apostle Paul, in writing to the Ephesian Christians, said, "Wake up! What's the matter with you? Stop acting like fools! Get your act together! Find out how God wants you to act!"

Actually, this is the way Paul put it:

> *Therefore He says: "Awake, you who sleep, Arise from the dead, And Christ will give you light." See then that you walk circumspectly, not as fools but as wise, redeeming the time, because the days are evil. Therefore do not be unwise, but understand what the will of the Lord is (Eph. 5:14-17).*

What is the will of the Lord? The answer follows in verse 18: "Do not be drunk with wine, in which is dissipation; but be filled with the Spirit."

What should Spirit-filled Christian husbands and wives be doing? "Speaking to one another in psalms and hymns and spiritual songs, singing and making melody in your heart to the Lord, giving thanks always for all things to God the Father in the name of our Lord Jesus Christ, submitting to one another in the fear of God" (Eph. 5:19-21).

Those who live without Christ don't know what it means to be grateful. We live in the most affluent culture in the history of the world, and Americans gripe and complain about everything and everyone — from the paperboy to the president.

And submissive? That's a dirty word. "No one's going to tell me what to do!" Everyone from toddlers to grandparents resists yielding their wills for the good of another. Rebellion is rampant, creating constant conflict at home, school, work, and in the streets. Why? Because people by nature are filled with self and not with the Spirit of God.

Let's look at the verbs at work in Ephesians 5:19-21: speaking, singing, making melody, giving thanks, and submitting.

Shouldn't Christians be different? Aren't we supposed to be doing the will of God? Think what a difference it would make in your marital relationship.

Husbands, how would you like to come home to a wife who's humming the latest praise tune while she's fixing dinner?

Wives, imagine your husband walking through the front door whistling the new chorus he learned at church last week?

What if the family's dinner conversation centered around the psalm you just read before blessing the food?

Wouldn't it be nice if before you went to bed at night, your husband said, "I'm so glad I married you," and you replied, "You're such a wonderful husband. I don't know what I did to deserve you"?

Husbands, how would you feel if the next morning your wife told you, "I've been thinking about your suggestion that we cut back on spending. This month I've decided to color my own hair instead of going to the salon."

What if he replied, "That's great, honey. By the way, this weekend I can build that new flower box you wanted."

Are you trying to do God's will? Do you have a song in your heart? Are you cultivating a submissive attitude and a thankful spirit in your home? Are you living to please God and your mate — or do you only think about your own feelings and happiness?

If you answered "no" to most of those questions, you need to change, but you can't do it on your own. You need the power of the Holy Spirit at work in your life.

How to Be Filled with the Spirit

One day my phone rang, and a lady said, "My husband is a minister. Would you counsel us and keep our meetings confidential?"

"Of course," I replied.

As soon as I met the husband, I knew he was a hard-driving, energetic choleric. It was easy to identify his temperament since I am one myself.

"We've been married 22 years," the wife began. "And I've had enough of his angry outbursts."

"What happened?" I inquired.

"He had a tremendous fist fight with our 19-year-old son. My husband was cruel and brutal, so I left him — temporarily. I agreed to return home if he would come with me for counseling."

I looked at him and said, "Sounds to me like you're a pretty angry man if these things are true. Are they?"

"Yes."

"Are you angry?" I asked.

"Well, Tim, you have to understand — a man has to have some place in life where he can relax and be himself."

Since I didn't know what to say, I was silent for a long time. Under the inspiration of the Holy Spirit, I shut my mouth and thought, *This very capable man is basically sincere.*

In the deafening silence, he got the message. Suddenly, he blurted out, "Gee, that sounds carnal, doesn't it?"

"Yes, it does," I replied. "May I suggest that when you relax and want to be your real self that you act with love, joy, peace, kindness, gentleness, goodness — that's the Holy Spirit."

"You're right," he replied meekly.

If you are not walking in the Spirit at home, you're walking in the flesh. When the apostle Paul said, "Walk in the Spirit," who do you think he was writing to? He was talking to born-again, former pagans — just like you and me. Many Christians tend to think that the Spirit-filled life is an option. "Do I want to be a Spirit-filled Christian or not?" they ask themselves. It's not an option — it's a command of God.

"I've tried," you say. "How can I walk consistently in the Spirit?"

Let me give you the same biblical formula I have shared with thousands of Christians.

First, examine yourself for sin. If you are indulging your emotions and giving into an area of weakness, you can change. Get this straight: You cannot walk in sin and walk in the Spirit at the same time.

If you have a pet sin, remember this verse, "Therefore we also, since we are surrounded by so great a cloud of witnesses, let us lay aside every weight, and the sin which so easily ensnares us, and let us run with endurance the race that is set before us" (Heb. 12:1). As a result of your inborn temperament, you have a tendency to sin in certain ways.

Some people have "the gift of criticism" — at least that's what they call it. Actually, they are critical people, and this sin is ruining their marriage relationship. Other people are undisciplined. Others are angry and cruel.

Some people are so passive, they are willing to sit back and let the world go by. These self-oriented, self-protected types avoid getting involved and simply let their mates handle every problem that comes along.

All of us have a tendency to fall into a sin pattern. You can be sure that Satan knows what it is, and he'll use your flesh and the world to tempt you every opportunity he gets. If you fall into that pattern, you cannot walk in the Spirit.

"How can I know what my sin pattern is?"

Every time you give in to some sin and the Holy Spirit convicts you, yield yourself to God and say, "Lord, is there some wickedness in my life?"

If you are regularly reading and studying God's Word and are open to hearing His voice, He will reveal the sin in your life. It will keep cropping up time and time again — in the pastor's sermon, in your devotional reading, on Christian radio — you won't be able to get away from God's convicting power.

Once you recognize the sin in your life, don't try to hide from it. Face it — no matter how ugly it may be — and take the next step.

Second, confess your sin. According to 1 John 1:9, "If we confess our sins, He is faithful and just to forgive us our sins and to cleanse us from all unrighteousness." Claim God's forgiveness through the shed blood of Jesus Christ. It doesn't do any good to keep beating yourself over the head. Jesus has already taken your punishment on the cross. Accept it and thank Him for forgiving you.

Third, yield your total self to God. Many sincere people confess their sin after they've faced it, but they never take all the wraps off and give themselves totally and completely to God.

The Bible commands us: "Offer yourselves to God . . . and offer the parts of your body to him as instruments of righteousness" (Rom. 6:13). You will never be filled with the Holy Spirit until you unreservedly give yourself to God as His possession.

We are commanded to love the Lord our God with all of our heart, all of our soul, all of our mind, and all of our strength (Mark 12:30). God tells us that He will not share our affection with another. He is a jealous God. He wants all of your heart — not 99.4 percent.

Fourth, ask to be filled with the Holy Spirit. Jesus said, "If you then, being evil, know how to give good gifts to your children, how much more will your heavenly Father give the Holy Spirit to those who ask Him!" (Luke 11:13).

Did He say, "Beg me," or "Tarry all night," or "Fast and pray"? No. "Ask," He said.

If you want to be filled with the Holy Spirit, meet His conditions and ask Him. Being filled with the Holy Spirit is a command, and God doesn't make His commands hard. All we have to do is receive His indwelling, controlling power. If you've never received the Holy Spirit into your life, I suggest you do so right now by asking Him to come in.

Fifth, believe that He's filled you with the Spirit. How do you know if you've been filled with the Holy Spirit? That is easy to tell. Just examine the life you live at home. If you have reflected the Spirit-filled life at home by the way you treat your spouse and your children, treating others with love and kindness out of a spirit of peace, that is the acid test.

If you have yielded yourself completely to God and asked Him to fill you with His Spirit, then trust Him that you are filled. Then thank Him for what He's done.

Sixth, enjoy life in the Spirit. When God fills us with His Spirit, He increases our joy, making us contagious to those around us. As a Spirit-filled believer, you will have a song in your heart, a thankful attitude, and a submissive spirit (Eph. 5:19-21).

Have you ever met a miserable thanker? I haven't. A person who is gratefully thanking God has a positive attitude about everything. When you're filled with the Spirit, you'll have a song in your heart, thanksgiving on your lips, and a submissive or cooperative attitude. Who wouldn't want to be married to a person like that?

Family

The Real Measure of Success

W e often hear of programs, techniques, and "gimmicks" that will help us keep our families on firm footing.

Sadly, these paths can lead to frustration rather than fulfillment for families because root issues aren't addressed. The heartbeat of the Bible is compassion, but many times, God's Word stands in the "tough love" camp.

In this section, Beverly LaHaye talks to wives about how God wants them to relate to their husbands.

When Tim was a young pastor, people often came to him with their problems. During the counseling session it would come out that they had already seen a professional counselor or psychiatrist.

"If you've been to a professional, why have you now come to see me?" Tim would ask.

They always had the same answer, "Because I ran out of money, and I know you're cheap."

Tim quit asking that question and decided instead to be thankful for the opportunity to point them in the right direction.

Today, Americans have access to all kinds of self-help books, tapes, and seminars. The professionals are out there ready to give their latest spin on how to be happily married and have a happy home life. All they have to offer, however, are suggestions.

The Bible, on the other hand, provides authoritative principles that have passed the test of time. After all, where did the concept of "family" originate?

It was God's idea. Our Heavenly Father performed the first marriage ceremony in the Garden of Eden and instituted the first family.

If God created the family, wouldn't He have the best advice on how a husband, wife, and children can live together in harmony?

The apostle Paul, in writing to the believers at Ephesus, succinctly provides a synopsis on successful Christian family living. In fact, Ephesians 5:18-6:18 presents the Bible's longest passage on family living.

The introduction to this passage in Ephesians deals with the Spirit-controlled life. What does that tell us? That instruction on the Spirit-filled life was given for the family. If we can live the Spirit-filled life at home, we can live it anywhere. After all, what we are at home portrays what we really are.

Be Controlled by the Holy Spirit

When you accept Jesus as your Saviour and make Him Lord, the Holy Spirit takes control of your life. In fact, we are commanded to "be filled with the Spirit" (Eph. 5:18).

How are you going to be different now that you are filled with the Spirit? These verses from Ephesians summarize how you will be changed once the Holy Spirit takes charge of your life:

 Speaking to one another in psalms and hymns and spiritual songs, singing and making
melody in your heart to the Lord, giving thanks always for all things to God the Father in the
name of our Lord Jesus Christ, submitting to one another in the fear of God (Eph. 5:19-21).

You'll have a song in your heart, thanksgiving in your soul, and a submissive spirit in all your relationships.

We are to submit ourselves to one another, to fellow believers in the body of Christ. Serving one another in love becomes our goal in life. Instead of the selfish attitude that once ruled our lives, we now ask, "How can I best help someone else?"

What a contrast to the attitude found in our society today, where most people ask, "What's in it for me?" Even couples entering into marriage often do so with selfish expectations, "What am I going to get out of this?" or "What can he do for me?"

Jesus taught us to be servants, and Scripture commands us "to serve one another" (Gal. 5:13). Instead of focusing on ourselves, we, as Christian wives, should be putting others first — especially at home.

Marriage is not a two-way relationship; it's a three-way relationship. When God is left out, the relationship loses its most stable leg. Before a marriage begins to fall apart, inevitably one or both partners have already thrown God out.

When the spiritual damage is repaired — and God is restored to His rightful place — then the couple has the divine resources to rebuild their marriage relationship.

Wives, Submit to Your Husbands

A well-known educational leader once told a group of college women that being a housewife is "an illegitimate profession." Women should "get out of the house and not be burdened with their children," she said. "Develop a profession, a career, so you can really make something of yourselves."

"Woman should not be under the leadership of the man," the feminists have insisted. "She should come out from under her husband's authority and be her own person." God's Word, however, makes it clear that He planned it differently:

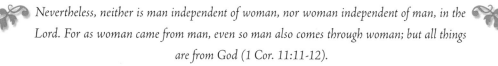

Nevertheless, neither is man independent of woman, nor woman independent of man, in the Lord. For as woman came from man, even so man also comes through woman; but all things are from God (1 Cor. 11:11-12).

Although the word "submission" has gotten a bad rap, it should carry a positive, not a negative meaning for women.

The fact is: Men need help! God knew it, and He created women to help them. That does not make women second-class citizens; it make us God's instruments to fulfill a particular role that helps keep God's creation running smoothly.

Family

Whenever a wife thinks she can switch roles with her husband, God's original design gets distorted. The result? A marriage in conflict and a family in chaos.

Wives, submit to your own husbands, as to the Lord. For the husband is head of the wife, as also Christ is head of the church; and He is the Savior of the body. Therefore, just as the church is subject to Christ, so let the wives be to their own husbands in everything
(Eph. 5:22-24).

The woman was designed and fashioned by God to make the husband a complete person. When husbands and wives walk together in unity, they help one another become better than either would have been without their mate.

Many women get hung up on "Wives, be in submission to your own husband," — and fail to see the most important part of this verse: "as to the Lord." When a wife comes to Jesus Christ, she submits herself to the Lord, knowing He will lovingly lead and care for her. In the same way, a wife can willingly submit to her husband.

A godly Christian husband will have the mind of Christ. "For the husband is head of the wife, as also Christ is head of the church; and He is the Savior of the body" (Eph. 5:23).

> "When husbands and wives walk together in unity, they help one another become better than either would have been without their mate."

My work as president of Concerned Women of America has brought me into contact with women from all walks of life, including many feminists. I have had the opportunity to observe these women on a personal and professional level and have found most feminists to be frustrated and hurting women.

Rejected, disappointed, and heartbroken, they often project their bitterness and resentment onto others. Unfortunately, this is the only way they know how to respond. Searching for love and freedom, they flounder, having refused their only hope for peace and fulfillment in this life. I urge you not to be deceived by the world's empty philosophy. It has nothing to offer us.

Beware lest anyone cheat you through philosophy and empty deceit, according to the tradition of men, according to the basic principles of the world, and not according to Christ (Col. 2:8).

God has already laid out His perfect plan for men and women and the family. If you return to the Word of God, you will find the way to personal happiness and a successful home life.

HUSBANDS, LOVE YOUR WIVES

Many women have had their homes torn asunder, or been rejected and experienced great disappointment, because their husbands did not know how to love. I have often wondered if there would be fewer feminists if they had married husbands who truly loved them "as Christ loved the church."

Husbands, love your wives, just as Christ also loved the church and gave Himself for her.... So husbands ought to love their own wives as their own bodies; he who loves his wife loves himself. For no one ever hated his own flesh, but nourishes and cherishes it, just as the Lord does the church (Eph. 5: 25-29).

Most wives would find it easy to submit to a husband who projects the loving humility and spiritual strength of the Lord as described in these verses. Imagine being loved as Christ loved the Church! I don't know any women who resist that kind of commitment, affection, and devotion.

Every husband needs to read and re-read these verses to remind himself to love his wife more than he loves his body — by nourishing and cherishing her. As Christ presents the Church spotless, without wrinkle

and blameless, so the husband is to build up his wife until he can present her in this manner. This is a beautiful picture indeed.

Accept the Uniqueness of the Marriage Relationship

Genesis 1 describes the origin of the family that began when God created man from the dust of the earth. Soon after this great creative miracle, God realized it was "not good for man to be alone." Man needed a helper — someone who would meet his needs and assist him in his journey through life.

Another Adam would not fit the bill, neither would a dog or horse or any other animal. God knew man needed a helper who would make Adam better than he could be on his own.

The second chapter of Genesis describes how God "fashioned" a woman taken from the man's rib. This newly created being, although different physically, psychologically, and emotionally, would fit the man like a hand in a glove. She was suitable for the man.

To emphasize the uniqueness of this man/woman relationship, the command was given: "For this reason a man shall leave his father and mother and be joined to his wife, and the two shall become one flesh" (Eph. 5:31).

In recent years, the simplicity and perfection of God's original plan for the family has come under attack and — in many homes — exists as a twisted and ugly mutation. The husband/wife relationship lost its uniqueness for many men and women when God's original command was rendered obsolete in modern society. Don't fall for that lie.

Accept and enjoy the uniqueness of the marriage relationship. There is nothing else like it. No other human relationship provides the intimacy and security of marriage. In a godly Christian marriage, you and your mate are free to be your best and to become all that God wants you to be. When that happens, everyone benefits — you, your mate, your children, and society in general.

Respect Your Husband

Tim once told me about a godly woman who was married to an alcoholic husband. Apparently, he stayed sober long enough to earn a living as a lawyer.

In spite of her husband's constant belittling of her faith, this woman raised four boys — and all of them graduated from Dallas Theological Seminary and entered the ministry.

One day Tim had the opportunity to meet this woman's youngest son and asked him, "What was it like growing up?"

"My dad ridiculed our faith and even tried to talk us out of believing in Jesus Christ," the young man said.

"With that kind of resistance, how did all four of you end up in the ministry?" Tim asked. "What was the secret?"

"It was my saintly mother," he replied with a smile. "She was a respected Bible teacher who taught 700 women in a Bible study. When my father would come home in a drunken stupor, she would go to the door and find him lying on the threshold. Many times he had thrown up all over his clothes. My mother would lovingly wash him off, put him into bed, and get him to sleep. She always treated him with dignity and respect and would never permit us to say anything bad about Dad. She always told us, 'Boys, he is your father.'"

These young men grew up to be like their mother, not their father.

Respect goes a long way in creating harmony in a home. That's why God gave us this command: "Nevertheless let each one of you in particular so love his own wife as himself, and let the wife see that she respects her husband" (Eph. 5:33).

If you want your husband to love you, you have to be careful how you act toward him. At all times, no matter how angry you get, always respect your husband, especially in front of your children. That means not criticizing him or tearing him down.

A husband who knows his wife loves and respects him will never have to look anywhere else for approval or affection. If he knows he can trust you, he will be free to share his heart with you.

Many wives complain that their husbands won't communicate with them on a meaningful level. One reason could be that husbands need to know you will listen without condemnation and that you won't repeat what he tells you. Also, keep in mind that men in general are not big talkers. In fact, Gary Smalley has noted that women speak 25,000 words a day while men only use about 12,000 words.

My husband, Tim, likes to tell the story about the man who heard that his dad was dying. He wanted to talk to him before he passed away, but he arrived a day late. When his brother met him at the airport, the man said, "I'm so sorry I didn't get here before Dad passed on. Did he have any last words?"

The brother replied, "No."

"Why not?" the man asked.

"Mama was with him right up to the end," the brother explained.

Maybe if we, as wives, talked less and listened more, our husbands' communication skills would improve!

In this section, Tim LaHaye provides interesting insights.

Your wife's wants — and needs — are different from yours. Why is that? First, because she is a woman, and women don't think like men. Women are wired differently. Secondly, her temperament type is different from yours.

Out of the 6,000 people I have counseled over the years, 4,000 of them had marital problems. In the process I learned a lot about both men and women, and I'm convinced that opposites attract. In fact, my wife and I are complete opposites when it comes to temperament.

Your wife's temperament will determine her priorities and what she wants from you. Don't be surprised if you find it confusing to fulfill her expectations. Since your wife's temperament may be opposite to yours, her expectations will naturally be different. Also, your priorities may not be the same as your wife's because priorities are determined by temperament.

That can be changed if you, as the husband, are willing to be the kind of man God wants you to be. As a man you come with a different set of spark plugs. Men have different needs. Once you understand God's role for you, however, you will be able to give your wife what she wants — and needs.

God's Word explains your responsibility as a husband:

> *Husbands, likewise, dwell with them with understanding, giving honor to the wife, as to the weaker vessel, and as being heirs together of the grace of life, that your prayers may not be hindered (1 Pet. 3:7).*

A Woman Wants to Be Respected

As a husband, you are to live together with your wife and honor her as "the weaker vessel." Where is she weak? In her emotions. That's why a man should never criticize his wife. Always honor her and build her up.

Some women, because of feminist indoctrination, have been brainwashed into thinking they have "come a long way, Baby." Feminists worship "self" and make self-assertiveness and self-actualization their main objectives in life.

A young woman may enter marriage with a defensive "You can't tell me what to do" attitude toward her husband. The older a woman gets, however, the more dependent she becomes on a man. Unfortunately, the converse is also true. If a wife dominates her husband in the early stages of marriage, then he'll be dependent on her later. It will also be difficult for her to accept her husband as the head of their household.

Respect her as a person. Why? Because she will accept herself according to the amount of respect you give her. The woman you married needs to be accepted regardless of how different she is from you. It's up to you to set the standard by respecting those differences.

Once you start showing respect for your wife, you must also demand that your children respect her. Kids aren't perfect either, and they are not going to automatically respect you and your wife. That's why God gave the command:

 Children, obey your parents in the Lord, for this is right. "Honor your father and mother," which is the first commandment with promise (Eph. 6:1-2).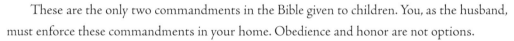

 Honor your father and your mother, that your days may be long upon the land which the Lord your God is giving you (Exod. 20:12).

These are the only two commandments in the Bible given to children. You, as the husband, must enforce these commandments in your home. Obedience and honor are not options.

I know that kids go through periods of rebellion when they outright refuse to submit to your authority as parents. During one difficult episode, one of our children wanted to move out and live with another family. "They're nicer than you are!" he said bluntly. You can imagine how that made us feel.

As the head of the house, the husband must set the standard by the way he talks to his wife and by what he expects of the children: "You will respect your mother, and you will respect me, whether you want to or not!"

Never, never, never let your kids sass or mouth their mother. Do not, under any circumstances, allow your children to "talk back" or verbally defy your wishes with, "I don't have to do what you say!" or "You're always on my back!"

Sure, it's easier to ignore such rude and challenging behavior with, "Well, he didn't really mean what he said," and refuse to correct the child. If you let it go, you are merely reinforcing the expressions of a rebellious heart.

At that point, you need to remind your child that he is disobeying God's command to "honor your father and mother." Then you should initiate the proper punishment in order to reinforce the fact that rebellion and disobedience will not be tolerated toward you or your wife.

When I was in fourth grade, I came home from school one day and said something smart-alecky and disrespectful to my mother. I don't remember what I said or why. I didn't realize that my dad was also home until I heard my name come flying out from the other room: "Tim!"

"Yes, sir?" I asked as I crept around the corner. My dad hadn't moved. His leg was still thrown over the arm of the chair. All he'd done was call my name.

"I want you to apologize to your mother for what you just said," he commanded. "And, young man, if I ever hear you speak like that to her again, there will be a hole in the wall just your size."

My mother died at 81, and I never spoke disrespectfully to her again. Why? My dad respected her and demanded that I respect her, too. What do you think that does for a woman? It makes her respect herself. And that's the greatest gift you could ever give your wife. My dad died when I was nine years old, but he taught me a lesson I never forgot — and one that I have taught to my own children.

A Woman Wants Love

Men want love in marriage, but love isn't as high a priority for them. Men are more sexually oriented, and that's natural and normal. A man's sex drive reaches its ultimate peak about the age of 21, then gradually tapers off after he's about 121, and then drops out of sight.

I started chasing the girls in the second grade. Until this very day my most difficult spiritual battle takes place in my mind. I work at keeping my thoughts pure by submitting my will to Jesus Christ — and it is a constant battle. One thing that helps me is to replace every unacceptable thought with something wholesome, because in the final analysis the battle is really won or lost in the mind. As the Bible teaches, as a man "thinks in his heart — so is he" (Prov. 23:7).

When I was a young preacher, an older pastor assisted me at a graveside funeral one day. I was so impressed with this 81-year-old man of God that I wanted his advice. "Brother Trotter, I need to ask you a question," I said. "How old do you have to get before you become, you know, before you get over being sexually tempted?"

He looked up at the sky and replied, "Brother LaHaye, I don't know. You'd have to be a lot older than I am."

That isn't exactly what I wanted to hear, but I realized I wasn't alone and that it was up to me to keep my desires under control.

Let's face it: men are sexually driven. Women are, too, at certain times, but their cycle is different from ours. A woman is sexually driven only about four to six days a month. A man's drive is more basic — like 58 days a month!

Women aren't sexually driven; they are motivated by love. They don't just want sex. Oh, sure, they enjoy it and even desire it once in a while, but sex doesn't drive them like it does us men. Many times a good wife will cooperate in sex because what she really wants is love, and that's what God wants you to give her — love!

Husbands, regardless of your temperament type or how old your wife is, my best advice to you is: Love her, love her, love her. Let her know that you love her as a person and that the person who inhabits her body is more important than the body.

When one of our church deacons and his wife celebrated 56 years of marriage, Bev and I stopped by their house to congratulate them. Unable to have any children, they cherished one another with an unusual and endearing love.

During our visit, I noticed an old, yellowing photograph taken of the wife on her wedding day. Pointing to the picture, I said, "Frank, your wife was a beautiful woman."

"Yes, Pastor, she was." Then a warm smile crossed his face, and he said, "But she's more beautiful to me today than she was back then."

I looked at that picture, and I looked at the elderly woman, and, I'll be honest, I couldn't see what he saw. Why? Because I was looking at the outer shell, her physical appearance, and he was looking at her heart. It was that inner woman that he loved, and he had always made her feel that she was the most wonderful woman in the world.

USA Today proposed this question to wives: "If you had it to do all over again, would you marry the same man?" Fifty-one percent said no. When men were asked the same question, 77 percent replied, "Yes, I would marry her again."

Then the wives were asked a second question: "Does your husband help you voluntarily around the house?" Out of the 49 percent who said, "Yes, I would marry the same man again" — 82 percent responded, "Yes, my husband helps out."

Were these wives more happily married because they had extra help at home? I don't think so. It was their husband's expression of love shown through his helpful actions that made the difference. Husbands, if you want to please your wife, find out what she hates to do around the house — and do it for her.

You know what my wife hates to do? She hates to empty the dishwasher after the dishes are clean. In fact, Bev will let the dirty dishes pile up before she'll bother to unload the dishwasher and put the clean dishes away.

When I see dirty dishes accumulating in the sink and on the counter, I make a point of unloading the dishwasher for her. Nothing pleases my wife more than to open the dishwasher and find it empty so she can start filling it up again. That's my simple way of saying, "I love you."

Men, you'll find that it doesn't take much to please your wife, especially if you do something without her having to ask you. One act of lovingkindness can speak a volume of "I love you's."

Since Bev has arthritis in one of her shoulders, pushing the vacuum cleaner is difficult for her. As for me, I hate vacuuming because my mother always made me do it when I was a kid. My aversion to vacuuming, however, has been replaced by the pleasure I get in seeing my wife's face light up when she walks into our condo, opens the door, and notices the clean carpet.

Of course, I've learned to make my efforts obvious by leaving wheel marks. After all, if I'm going to do it, I might as well let it show!

Your love, expressed in words and deeds, makes your wife feel good about herself as a person. When she feels loved and accepted, she no longer has to demand your affection and attention. Men are different. We can find our self-acceptance in other areas.

Whatever your job, if you do it well, and your boss pats you on the back and, particularly, if he gives you a raise, you feel good about yourself because men are vocationally oriented.

Athletics also boosts our self-esteem. That's why men can't resist a backyard game of football — even if it means risking life and limb. Some men keep trying to be a stud at 30 and 40 and 50 when they should give it up. There's something about physical activity that builds us up as a man.

Fatherhood has huge impact on our sense of manliness. Simply fathering a child, however, doesn't make a man a good father.

What makes a woman feel good about herself? Her husband. She receives her self-acceptance from you. If she feels only disapproval coming from you, she will be depressed and insecure. Even if she's the best lawyer in the town or the best doctor at the hospital, when your wife comes home she will feel inadequate if she senses your disapproval.

If you are a perfectionist, you probably have unrealistic expectations for your wife to meet. When she doesn't measure up to your impossible standards, you withhold your approval. Your wife will either drive herself crazy striving to be perfect or give up and live in a constant state of depression.

Men have a tendency to want to keep their wives guessing. In some sadistic way, we think that keeps them on their toes. Actually, all it does is lower her self-esteem and make her feel insecure.

Remember, she is the "weaker vessel." Emotionally, she desperately needs to be constantly reassured that you truly love her — not just on your anniversary or Valentine's Day, but every day. As her husband, you must regularly communicate to her, "Honey, I love you so much that if I had it to do all over again, you would still be my first choice."

A WOMAN WANTS COMPANIONSHIP

Your wife wants to become your best friend. I use the word "become" because it takes time. If you are a young married couple, don't be surprised if your wife isn't your best friend, yet.

I have found that Christian couples have a huge advantage in this area of marital friendship. Why? Because the husband and wife already share the most important bond between them — their faith in Jesus Christ. As a result, they have similar goals in life. Even if they have vastly different careers and interests, they share one overwhelming objective: to live a life pleasing to God. This puts Christian couples way ahead of the game.

Add to that the fact that their social and spiritual life usually revolves around the church. This is where they develop friendships with other couples and participate in many activities together. The church and the overall Christian community provide an arena of commonality that bonds believers together as no other organization or social group can.

That doesn't mean that Christian couples agree on everything. I had a secretary many years ago who was very conservative (she had to be to work for me). Her husband, however, was a liberal Democrat. They got along great until the elections rolled around.

During the Bush/Dukakis presidential election, their relationship was particularly strained. On election night, my secretary's husband was listening to the voting results on his way home from work. Dukakis was going down in flames, making him more and more depressed.

When he arrived home, his wife — overjoyed that George Bush was winning — walked over to greet him. "You're finally home," she smiled, waiting for her good evening greeting and kiss.

The guy looked at her and walked right by without saying a word. Stunned, she asked, "What's wrong?"

"I'm just not ready to kiss a Republican yet."

While some couples can allow for personal preferences and even dramatic differences of opinion, it doesn't make for smooth sailing. The more areas of commonality that a husband and wife share, the sweeter their marital friendship blossoms.

During the years when my wife spent most of her time caring for our four children, she had very little time to read books or articles. To make matters worse, she and I have different sleeping habits. Bev is an early-to-bed and early-to-rise person. I'm just the opposite — I do my best work at night and in the morning wake up like death warmed over. That fact alone could create serious problems in a marriage relationship.

As a minister, I was constantly reading and trying to keep up with the latest social and religious issues. In the evening, after dinner when the kids were in bed, my wife would fall asleep with a book in her lap. After all, it was 8:30 at night — twilight zone for Bev.

This went on for about ten years. She wasn't doing much reading, and I noticed that we were drifting apart mentally. We were no longer on the same wavelength.

Troubled, I began to pray about the situation, and God opened my eyes. I noticed that Bev had an incredible memory. Whenever I told Bev about a book I had been reading, she could still recall it months later. I decided to begin sharing more information with her since she didn't have time to read herself.

One day I heard Bev explaining, almost word for word to a friend, facts I had long forgotten. I'm convinced she has a better memory than I do.

As a couple, you need to make sure you are both on the same page. If your wife is lagging behind, bring her along beside you. If your husband gets too far ahead of you, try to catch up. When you are on long drives together, listen to the same music or the same messages. Then discuss how the words or teaching applies to your lives and relationships.

The more areas of commonality you can develop, the more you will enjoy each other's companionship. Your marriage will be enriched, and your friendship will grow.

A Woman Wants a Family

Most men also want children, but a wife *needs* a family. Before contraceptives and abortion, women didn't have much control over how many children they birthed. As a result, it was not unusual for a family to enjoy five, six — even ten children. Today, the average American family has only one or two children.

I often tell newly married couples, "Have as many children as you can raise to love and serve God." Why? Because the older you get, the more you realize that the most important thing in your life is your family.

Over the years, I have written more than 50 books (some are best sellers) and that gives me a tremendous sense of accomplishment. My greatest enjoyment in life, however, has come from our four children. Three are involved in Christian ministry.

> "While some couples can allow for personal preferences and even dramatic differences of opinion, it doesn't make for smooth sailing. The more areas of commonality that a husband and wife share, the sweeter their marital friendship blossoms."

Even today, Bev and I enjoy nothing more that being with our children and their families. In fact, we plan our schedules so we can spend vacations and holidays with some of the most important people in the world — our children and grandchildren. That's how important family is to us.

Cultivate your family by spending as much time together as possible. Learn to enjoy one another now, and you'll pave the way for many future years of happiness.

A Woman Wants a Leader

Every wife — no matter what her temperament — needs a husband who will take the lead and be head of their family.

If your wife has a choleric temperament, you may need to give her a little more room to express herself. If you impose your will arbitrarily, she will become totally frustrated. Give her the opportunity to give her opinion, but it is up to you as the husband to make the final decision.

I have a friend who was intimidated by his wife's strong will. When he came to me for counseling, I told him "Let your wife express herself, thank her for her opinion, and then you decide what is best for the family. But don't squelch her need to verbalize what she thinks."

Most women want a man who is going to lead. In the ideal situation, corporate decisions are made in which you decide together what to do in a given situation. Usually, however, one mate has to submit to the other partner.

When someone has to be the decision maker, it should be the husband. That's your job; it goes with the territory. You won't always be popular, but in the long run, even if your wife and kids disagree with the decision, they will respect the fact that you were man enough to make it.

As a father, I had to make many difficult decisions. The major ones I submitted to God, and the results were positive. On the minor decisions, I thought, *I can decide this myself* — and those were my biggest mistakes. Fortunately, God is a master at picking up the pieces and putting them back together again.

At 15 years of age, during a Christian summer camp, I gave my life to Jesus Christ for the gospel ministry.

Later I became enamored with becoming a lawyer, so I tried bargaining with God. "If you let me go to law school," I promised, "I'll come back and become the district attorney of Detroit and clean up the city."

God had other plans for my life, and I'm glad He led me into the ministry. It has not only been rewarding, it has been fun. God's will always turns out right.

Whenever you have to make a major decision in life, get alone with God and lay out your concerns before Him. Then pray, "Lord, this is what I'd like to do, but I know that You have a will for my life, and I want You to guide me to do the right thing."

When a difficult family decision — big or small — has to be made, pray for wisdom to judge the matter fairly. Then ask God to give you the strength to stand by your decision. The more unpopular the decision, the more graciously you need to present it to your family. Do it resolutely without backing down, no matter how much opposition you face. Remember, you are responsible to God to be the leader of your household.

During our family life seminars, I often suggest to those attending that they write down any questions they want me to answer. One of the top five questions — from among the hundreds that are asked every year — comes from wives who ask: "How can I get my husband to be the spiritual leader of our family?"

What is a spiritual leader? A man who is spiritually minded himself and who leads his family in spiritual growth. I hope you have a time, at least four or five days a week, when you lead your wife and children in family devotions. All it takes is ten minutes out of your busy day to read a small portion of Scripture and pray together about the needs of your family. By your example, you set the spiritual pace for your children to follow — whether it is prayer, daily Bible reading, or church attendance.

In addition to family-time prayer, the husband and the wife need to pray together concerning issues that affect you as a couple.

Many years ago, Bev was asked to appear before the Senate judiciary committee confirmation hearing for Judge Robert Bork. Naturally, she was very nervous. It must be pretty intimidating to speak for five minutes in front of well-known senators like Ted Kennedy, Joe Biden, and others.

As Bev was hurrying out of the house, I could tell she was nearly overwhelmed by the tremendous responsibility facing her. I took her in my arms and prayed for God to give her peace and wisdom.

Later, a federal judge in Asheville, Kentucky, who had come to a men's seminar where I was speaking, came to me afterward and asked, "Would you give a message to your wife? I caught her testimony at the judiciary committee for the appointment of Judge Bork, and I thought she did a superb job." Actually, she did a supernatural job because of the grace of God.

When your wife faces difficult situations that press her to the limit of her abilities and talents, you need to be there supporting her. That is not the time for an ego trip on your part. That's the time to act like a man, take her in your arms, and say, "I'm here for you, sweetheart. Let me pray for you. I know you'll do great!" Your wife needs to know that you support her spiritually.

A Woman Wants Happiness

Every person who has ever come to me for counseling had the same problem: They were miserable. I've never had anyone come in for marriage counseling and say "Pastor LaHaye, we are so happy we just can't stand it. Could you help us?"

No. It's always been the opposite. "We have made each other miserable." No one gets married to become miserable. Every bride thinks she has found Mister Right, and he is going to make her happy forever after. It doesn't work that way. All those people who needed counseling because they were miserable had one thing in common: They had earned the right to be miserable. Why? Because they had broken the principles of God.

More than once, a woman would tell me about this brute she married and how he's mistreating her. When I ask her why she married him, she says, "I married an unbeliever against my parents' wishes."

What's wrong with wanting happiness? Isn't that what we're here for? Every human being wants happiness, and as Christians we have the greatest resource on happiness in the world — the Bible.

Did you know that the word "blessed" really means happy? Jesus said, "I've come that you might have life and that you might have it" — how? — "more abundantly." Jesus makes everything more abundant.

I took a sex survey of 3,404 people and discovered that Christians have the highest level of sexual satisfaction and frequency than any other segment in our society. We don't brag about it, we don't talk about it, we don't read dirty books about it, we just go on enjoying it year after year after year, more than any group in our culture.

The world has a twisted view of sex because they think that the physical experience on a human level is all there is to it. Christians, however, involve the spiritual part of our lives, and that enriches everything.

What is the secret to happiness? Jesus gave it when He said, "Blessed are those who hear the word of God and keep it" (Luke 11:28). "Blessed" is another word for happy.

As a husband and father, the head of your household, you need to make this commitment: *My family is going to follow Jesus Christ. We're going to obey the Word of God.* If you do that, you will be a happy husband with a happy wife and happy children.

I hope you'll invest yourself in the greatest institution in your life — your family.

In this section, Beverly LaHaye returns to Ephesians 6 for tips on family life and raising children.

One Sunday morning after church, a lady from our congregation came by and grabbed my husband's hand.

"Pastor," she begged earnestly, "would you promise to pray for our family every day?"

"Why, Sylvia?" Tim asked.

"Our youngest child just turned 13," she moaned, "and I realize we now have three teenagers all at the same time!"

Tim was so impressed by her request that on the way home he told me about the incident. I turned and looked at him rather strangely. "Tim, don't you realize that we have four?"

A panicked look came across his face as he realized we needed more prayer support than Sylvia!

Every father and mother wants to be a good parent, but anyone who has children knows it isn't an easy assignment.

WHERE SHOULD WE TURN FOR ADVICE?

A Christian insurance man once told Tim, "I used to give Dr. Spock's books on childrearing to anyone who bought insurance or any clients who had a new baby."

Tim and I couldn't understand why until we realized that back in those days, there was very little teaching on raising children — or on marriage and family life in general.

After 30 years of teaching Spockism and permissiveness and "don't spank your children," Dr. Benjamin Spock himself, at 76 years of age, publicly announced on television, "I made a mistake. You should discipline your children. You should teach them responsibility."

Guess what? The Bible has been teaching that for millenniums.

Let's go back to Ephesians 6 for instructions on how children and parents can live happily together.

Children, Obey Your Parents

 Children, obey your parents in the Lord, for this is right. "Honor your father and mother," which is the first commandment with promise: "that it may be well with you and you may live long on the earth" (Eph. 6:1-3).

Children need to be under the authority of their parents. They need our love, our guidance, our wisdom, and our protection.

At the same time, children need to honor their parents. In fact, as parents we do our children a favor by making them honor and obey us. Why? So they can enjoy the promises of God. What could be better than for your children to have everything in their lives go smoothly? What greater gift than to have your child enjoy a full, rewarding, and long life?

Without proper training in respect and discipline, a child grows up without self-control or self-respect. This leaves him vulnerable to his own childish whims and desires.

Did you know that more teenagers today die in accidents of one kind or another than from any other cause of death? Suicide also ranks high on the death list. It's a dangerous world out there, and you do your child no favors by letting him do as he pleases.

My husband Tim relates an incident that makes this point quite well:

One day, when I was 17 years old, my mother told me, "Tim, God spoke to me about you this morning in my devotions."

I always hated to hear her say that. I remember praying, "Lord, quit sending messages by my mother. Send them direct."

Then she pulled out her Bible and read. "Evil companions corrupt good morals," she quoted. "Son, I've come to the conclusion that those four boys you've been running around with are having a bad influence on you."

I couldn't believe it. "But, Mom, you want me to break off with friends I've played sports with through junior and senior high," I complained. "If I do that I won't have *any* friends."

"Yes, you will," she said. "I want you to go down to the church and make new friends."

"I don't even like those guys. They're a bunch of sissies!" For the first time in my life, I defied my mother — who had been a widow since I was nine years old. Politely and respectfully, I said, "Mom, I won't do it. They've been my friends too long. I will not do it."

At just five feet tall, she pounded on the table with her bony little finger and said, "Young man, as long as you park your feet under my table, you will abide by my rules. You either break off with those friends or you leave home."

I left home — for two days. Nobody would feed me, so I came back.

My mother met me at the door and asked, "On my terms?"

"Yeah, Ma, on your terms."

Thank God, I had a mother who could see where I was headed. I would have destroyed myself. I later learned that one of those four former friends spent 16 years in the federal penitentiary. Two of them have been married and divorced three times.

As for me, I went on to serve the Lord as a pastor and marry a wonderful wife. I am what I am today because my mother had the courage to stand on God's Word and not back down in the face of my defiance.

By the way, some of my best friends today are the guys I met at the church.

Left to himself, a child will never have the inner strength and will power to resist peer pressure, drugs, alcohol, sex, or any other sin.

Back in 1979, during the International Year of the Child, we first began to hear about "children's rights" and "the child advocacy laws." Secular humanists were advocating that children should have the right to sexual activity, to their own finances, and even the right to vote. Why? Because they are human beings.

Children in America today face issues that didn't even exist 20 years ago. As a parent, you must continuously be aware of how you can best meet your children's needs today — lest they be lost in the conflict.

FATHERS, DON'T PROVOKE YOUR CHILDREN

 Fathers, do not provoke your children to wrath, but bring them up in the training and admonition of the Lord (Eph. 6:4).

In other words, Dad, don't be so unreasonable that your children become totally frustrated. Use common sense when you make your rules and decide on punishments. Treat your children the way you like to be treated. Don't use your position of authority over them to demean them psychologically or harm them physically. If you do, they will become exasperated and lose all respect for you.

The responsibility for training and discipline is given to fathers. Why? Because husbands who are also fathers are the head of the family and carry the responsibility for training and disciplining the children.

This does not mean that Mom should sit idly by and tell the child, "Wait 'til your father gets home!" It does mean that the wife enforces the rules and standards of discipline determined by her husband.

FAMILIES, BE STRONG IN THE LORD

Since the apostle Paul has been talking about household issues in Ephesians 5 and 6, it is reasonable to assume that Ephesians 6:10 is also addressed to family members.

The word "finally" tells us that Paul is summing up everything he has already said: "Finally, my brethren, be strong in the Lord, and in the power of his might."

Yet, what's happening in our society today? Families are torn apart, divorce rates increase every year, young people run away from home, children rebel against parents, and the family unit becomes weaker and weaker. Why? Because we've let down our guard.

How can we strengthen our families? By putting on "the full armor of God that you may be able to stand firm against the schemes of the devil" (Eph. 6:11). What is the "full armor of God"? God's Word.

You cannot raise children today, have a strong family, and resist all the schemes of the devil and society without the authority of the Word of God.

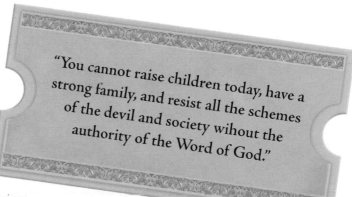

"You cannot raise children today, have a strong family, and resist all the schemes of the devil and society wihout the authority of the Word of God."

We are living in evil days. Children are being pulled away from parental guidance and taught things that are contrary to God's Word.

America's public school system teaches our children to deny God as their Creator by presenting evolution as fact instead of theory. The schools have usurped parental authority in many areas, including the right of the parent to teach their children about proper sexual behavior.

As a parent, you need to re-stake your claim and stand your ground. Instill proper moral values and conviction in your children. Have regular times of family Bible study. Be strong in the Lord. Rescue your children from the enemy's clutches before it is too late.

Parents, Stand Firm against Sin

 Therefore take up the whole armor of God, that you may be able to withstand in the evil day, and having done all, to stand (Eph. 6:13).

Let's look at some specific areas where we, as Christian parents, need to take a firm stand.

• **Drugs and alcohol.**

I recently read an article about fourth grade children who were becoming alcoholics and drug addicts. Why is this happening in our society? Some children are simply following their parents' example. Television also makes drinking look glamorous. Macho men take a beer can and crush it with their hands while lovely ladies hold martinis in their hand.

This one-sided view fails to present the harsh reality to children: Alcohol destroys lives and families. Television needs to show the broken homes, the mothers and children beaten up by alcoholic fathers, the child's wagon crushed by the roadside after being hit by a drunken driver.

Don't expect society to teach your children not to drink alcohol. You, as Christian parents, must take a firm stand against it and follow through with strict punishment if your child disobeys. Set the standard and enforce it with your teenagers. You may save his or her life if you do.

• **X-rated movies and television programs.**

Immorality has flooded into America's living rooms. With one click of the remote, adultery, sexually explicit behavior, profanity, blasphemy — filth we would never tolerate in person — infiltrate our lives under the guise of sitcoms, humor, drama, and mystery.

Like a computer, our minds absorb everything we take in through our eyes and ears and store it away in different files. Whenever a situation arises, that file comes up and influences how we will act at the moment.

If your children are watching hours and hours of sexually explicit movies and TV sitcoms, guess where that information is being stored. In their minds. Guess how they will act when a tempting situation arises.

Why do you think teen sex and teen pregnancies are so common? Because kids and teens have been programmed by what they see and hear to act and react accordingly.

It's up to you as a parent to take a strong stand against immorality, and the place to begin is in your own family room.

• **The homosexual/lesbian agenda.**

What is their agenda? To suck as many children as possible into their filthy pit.

Make no mistake about it. They are out to trap your children. They have already infiltrated the schools with explicit teaching about their "alternative lifestyle."

This so-called "gay" lifestyle has nothing to do with happiness. Sadness and heartache always result when anyone disobeys God's commands regarding sexual purity. AIDS and other sexually transmitted diseases have already taken a toll in America.

Most homosexuals were lured into this debilitating lifestyle because of a sexual encounter during childhood, and it was often with a friend, relative, or baby sitter.

Always know where your children and teenagers are and who they are with. You can never be too careful.

These are only a few of the temptations your children face on a daily basis. As adults, we have more freedom to remove ourselves from unpleasant or ungodly activity. Kids and teens, however, are bombarded by wickedness day after day. That's why you need to make your home a place of refuge. Monitor which programs your children watch on TV, refuse to allow secular music, and get acquainted with their friends.

If you don't fight for your family, who will? You must take an active part in our children's defense. Unless you and I stand up and speak out against these sins in our society, as the Word of God teaches, our children or our children's children will certainly be overwhelmed in the enemy's wake.

Pray at All Times

When should we pray? "Praying always with all prayer and supplication in the Spirit" (Eph. 6:18).

Pray for your children, your husband, and your wife. Pray for our nation, our schools, and our government officials. Pray whenever you see evil gaining ground. Be on the alert against new attacks. Don't stick your head in the sand and pretend that the evil of our day will somehow vanish.

It takes courage and perseverance to build a strong family today, but it can and is being done in homes all across America.

Tim and I had the opportunity to meet Dr. Frances Schaeffer before his death. This great man of God made a tremendous impact on his generation. He made a statement that will ring in our ears for years to come: "He that will not use his freedom to preserve his freedom will lose his freedom, and neither his children nor his children's children will rise up to call him blessed."

Dr. Schaeffer put those words into action. In his dying days — in fact, ten days before he succumbed to the cancer that was eating at his body — he picketed an abortion clinic. Why? Because he wanted to preserve the freedom of speaking out for the unborn children.

"Pay close attention to great men and women of God in their dying days," Dr. Schaeffer told his children and grandchildren, "because very often their last words will be a great message that you must heed."

What were Dr. Frances Schaeffer last words to his family? "Do not give up the fight; keep on praying; keep on fighting."

That's what God is saying to us as Christian parents today: "Keep praying and fighting for your family."

In this section, Tim LaHaye explains how humanism affects America's children and what you can do to protect them.

WHERE THE BATTLE RAGES

Why are Americans losing the battle for the family? Why is family life in such jeopardy today? The answers lie in the conflict between two major ideologies.

WHAT IS SECULAR HUMANISM?

What is the most powerful philosophy in America today? Secular humanism. In fact, the only group capable of resisting the humanist onslaught is born-again Christians who know their Bible.

Based on the idea that "man is the measure of all things," humanism promotes these basic principles: atheism, no God, and evolution.

Educators and academicians love the theory of evolution. Why? Because it justifies man's origin without God. If they can explain away God, then they don't have to answer to Him, or so they reason.

What makes evolution so dangerous? If you teach a generation of people that they are animals, pretty soon they will start acting like animals, and animals are universally amoral. They are not created in the image of God, as man is, nor do they have a moral consciousness.

Only the Bible teaches that man has an inborn conscience that either accuses or excuses us. If we do right, we feel good about ourselves. When we do wrong, we feel bad.

Why do people have a guilt neurosis? Because they're guilty. Only those who believe in the death and resurrection of Jesus Christ can confess their sin and be forgiven of it. Why? Because God's Word says, "If we confess our sins, He is faithful and just to forgive us our sins and to cleanse us from all unrighteousness" (1 John 1:9).

God removes our transgression as far as the east is from the west, and our sin will never again be remembered against us.

> "How can we strengthen our families? By putting on 'the full armor of God that you may be able to stand firm against the schemes of the devil'" (Eph. 6:11).

Neither Freud nor Skinner nor any humanist psychologist or psychiatrist can remove your guilt. All they can do is try to talk you out of it — after all, there is no right or wrong in their eyes. That's why so many people are depressed today. They have no way to resolve their feelings of guilt.

This puts kids in tremendous jeopardy, because young people, more so than adults, don't know how to handle their guilt. As a result, they sink into deep depression and many times never recover. This is one reason the suicide rate among teens is so high. They see no way out, and hopelessness eventually overwhelms them to the point of taking their own lives.

Trapped in the Sexual Revolution

At school and through the media, the humanists bombard children with blatant messages encouraging free sex.

"You need to learn how to use your bodies and practice your sexuality," kids are told, long before they are mature enough to bear the responsibilities of their deeds. "Don't worry about your parents. They're just out of touch."

Parents want their children to be moral, but educators think they know best: "Bring in Planned Parenthood." Now there's a con job.

After decades of Planned Parenthood's influence in America's schools, what did we get? A teenage pregnancy rate that increases every year, making it the number one social problem in our nation today.

Add to that the lie of "safe sex," and what happens? An epidemic of AIDS and STDs that is devastating a generation of young people like the plague.

What is the natural result of this sexual revolution? Teaching amorality has corrupted a generation and destroyed family life in America. Chastity before marriage and faithfulness to one mate has become obsolete. Many kids today have never even heard those words.

When they do get married, they usually don't last. Why? Because all they've been taught is how to have sex — not how to build a marriage relationship. In fact, the most common marital destroyer today is infidelity, either physical or mental.

Anyone who indulges in sexual fantasies long enough will eventually act it out. Infidelity damages a marriage more quickly and more completely than any other sin. Why? Because marriage is a sexual contract. When two people become one, they pledge themselves, as long as they both live, to keep that contract. Such pledges mean little to a generation that has had no limits placed on sexual activity.

The American Mindset

People like to say that we live in a pluralistic society. As far as I know there are only two major plurals: secular humanist thought and the Judeo-Christian moral ethic.

Although our country was founded on biblical principles, the humanists, in the last century, have taken over the media, the government, the public school system, and a number of important organizations. As a result, a mere 10 or 15 percent of our population has a controlling influence on 90 percent of our culture.

The humanists have come along and said, "Anything goes. Make up your own mind. There's no one up there telling you what's right and wrong."

Man's wisdom centers on atheism, evolution, and amorality, because these theories put man at the center of his autonomous, self-centered world view.

That's the mindset that many Americans have adopted. It's preached at us day after day, hour after hour — over the radio, in music, by the news media, in TV sitcoms, and documentaries. Even the Discovery Channel, the Animal Planet, and Public Broadcasting propagate the theory of evolution, and their belief that man is an animal.

The media has brainwashed an entire generation, and American culture is paying the price.

CIRCLE THE WAGONS!

I've lived in Southern California long enough to know that most of the evils affecting our society emanate from Hollywood and permeate throughout the United States. We have a culture that is working insidiously to destroy the family.

With God's help, you can still have a happy marriage, a good family, and raise children to love and serve God — even in this hostile culture of ours. If that is your goal, however, you will need tremendous determination. If you don't make family living, marriage, and child raising your highest priority — and spend more time at it than your parents did — you'll lose your children.

We are losing them. In the evangelical churches today, we are losing between 35 and 50 percent of our young people to the world before they graduate from high school. Why? Because of the cultural evils and the lack of protection around the home.

It's not too late. As parents, you can keep that from happening by building "rings of insulation" around your family to keep out society's insidious forces. It's time to circle the wagons.

PROVIDE A SAFE REFUGE FOR YOUR CHILDREN

In American society today, it is nearly impossible to escape the barrage of humanist deception and lies.

Did you know that in the last 30 years Christianity has more than doubled in our country? In fact, church growth has almost tripled.

As Bev and I travel across the United States, we find many large churches with hundreds of members where the Bible is being preached. People are being drawn to the truth, and the Holy Spirit is speaking to hearts and blessing families.

At the same time, the humanist influence on our culture has promoted a downsurge in moral values. We are closer to Sodom and Gomorrah today than we were 30 years ago. Why? Because Christians have abandoned the most influential arenas — the media, government, and secular education — the places where public opinion is formed.

There is a place of refuge. It's in your home and your church. Thankfully, Christian media — television, videos, radio, and music — is becoming stronger and providing alternatives.

It's up to parents, however, to set the example by what you read, watch, and listen to. Then you can encourage your kids to do the same.

Get involved in your children's education. Home school them if necessary, or make the financial sacrifices necessary to send them to Christian school.

If your child has a humanistic education, his view of God, creation, mankind, and himself will be distorted. This will affect his goals in life and how he treats other people.

If your child has a biblically based Christian education, he will learn to value the principles of integrity, humility, service, and love taught by Jesus Christ.

An important, but often overlooked, way to protect your family and children's future requires your involvement in the political process. You need to be a registered voter, and you need to vote in every election of our governing officials, from the local tax collector to the president.

Christians also have a responsibility to vote for people who share their moral values. Former Vice President Quayle, whom I know to be a born-again Christian, was right when he said we are in a great cultural divide between the elite in the media, education, and government. They are on one side, and the rest of America is on the other.

Our Christian founding fathers gave us the greatest nation on earth, one that has provided more freedom to more people for a longer period of time than any other in history. Liberal secular humanists are destroying our once-Christian culture due to the apathy of the 52 percent of Christians who do not even vote.

I believe God will hold us accountable for our lack of Christian responsibility for not voting into office those who share our moral values. In a republic, we deserve the kind of government we get, by voting or not voting. The very least we can do for our children is try to vote into office men and women who make good moral role models.

GIVE YOUR KIDS A LOVING HOME

Parents, I hope that you'll make every effort to love not only each other, but also your children.

One tangible way to show your love is to reach out and touch them. Christian psychologist John Trent suggests that every child needs about 25 touches a day — and every partner, particularly every wife, needs at least 12 touches every day.

Men, don't wait until ten o'clock at night and then give your touches all at once.

A touch is an identification. When you reach out to a child or your mate, you are saying, "You are special to me." As you pass by your son or daughter and gently touch his or her shoulder, you let that child know, "You are very special to me."

Children who are loved grow up to have greater self-worth. If a young person comes from a broken home or from a love-starved family where they don't feel accepted, that affects how they view themselves.

Our world is starving for love. Children have a natural desire to want to believe "My parents love me."

I was raised in a very poor family. My father died when I was nine years old, leaving my mother a widow with three little children. My brother was only seven weeks old at the time. Without any income, my mother had to trust God.

Financially, our family had some very grim years, but as I look back on my childhood, I think I was rich. Why? Because I knew what it meant to be loved.

You may have been raised in the lap of luxury, but if you didn't have love, you were cheated out of life's most important gift.

I look back and think, *My mom and dad dearly loved me.* I was important to them. That's the greatest gift you can give your children. Take time to love every member of your family each day.

Take Them to a Bible-Teaching Church

The church you attend is the best friend your family has. I have seen from experience that the strongest and the best families attend church. The church is the one organization in our culture that supports the values you are trying to inoculate into your children. Your church provides sound Bible teaching for the entire family, from the nursery children and primaries through junior high and high school.

Is church attendance necessary? Yes, if you want to obey God's Word, which teaches us not to forsake "the assembling of yourselves together" (Heb. 10:25).

"But my kids are at that age when they don't want to go," you say. Take them with you anyway.

Some Christian families have an election on Saturday night. Are we going to go to church tomorrow? That's spiritual suicide.

Raise your kids with this understanding, "Unless you have a communicable disease that will endanger somebody else's health, we all go to church on Sunday." It isn't a matter of *you* go, it's *we* go.

In essence, you are saying, "Follow me as I follow Christ."

Teach Your Child That He Is Unique

Every child is unique and is born with a certain temperament. If you are an introvert, you were born an introvert. If you are an extrovert, you were born an extrovert. Temperament accounts for 20 to 30 percent of your child's behavior.

A few years ago, I was introduced to a psychologist, who blatantly asked: "Oh, you're the guy who speaks on temperament, aren't you?"

"Yes," I replied.

"I think that's a lot of bologna!" he quipped.

"Well," I replied, "last night I attended our church's pre-school Christmas program and made an interesting observation."

"Really?" the psychologist asked.

"When the little ones had assembled on stage, I noticed a little boy — I'll call him Johnny — in the back row, stretching his neck and looking over the faces in the audience. Finally, he spotted his dad and shouted, 'Hi, Dad!' as he waved and jumped in an effort to be seen.

"A little girl on the front row also caught my eye, same size and age as the uninhibited boy in the back row. Suzy shuffled to her place with downcast eyes. Obviously petrified by the crowd, she reached down for the little tassel on her dress, pulled it up, and put it in her mouth.

"Now, Doctor," I proceeded to ask, "do you mean to tell me that the different types of behavior exhibited by those toddlers was learned in only two years, or was it born in them?"

Fifty years from now, Johnny will still be outgoing and uninhibited, but hopefully not obnoxious. Suzy, although probably more sure of herself by then, will have retained her demure and reserved personality.

One young mother, whose toddler had an unmistakable choleric temperament, told me, "He gets into everything and won't sit still for a minute." When I asked her about his conduct in the womb, she answered, "He kicked every organ in my body!"

My mother said the same. Maybe yours did, too.

God blessed Bev and I with four children — two boys and two girls. They are so different we often wonder if they are really ours! Although they were formed from the same gene pool, each one has distinct physical features and a unique temperament. It's something that came with them at birth.

Sometimes when parents introduce me to their son, I can't help but wonder, *Could this kid have come from these parents? He must be adopted.* Then at a later time, I will meet the boy's grandfather and realize, *This kid is a dead ringer for his granddad!*

No wonder. After all, we come from two parents and four grandparents, who have all contributed genes to our makeup, both physical and temperamental. At least six people, and maybe some great-grandparents, supply components of our nature.

Most people are a combination of two or more temperaments — a strong one and a secondary. Other factors also affect the way your child thinks and acts. Childhood training, habits, education, self-discipline, motivation, mental attitude, and health all affect his behavior.

In school, the Sparky Sanguine kid usually functions between D- and F, but still thinks he's Mr. Wonderful. Sanguines especially need to cultivate self-discipline.

The Melanie Melancholy kid regularly gets A's and B's. If she gets an A-, she's depressed. "Oh, I didn't get a perfect score."

Whatever your child's temperament, try to identify it, accept the strengths and weaknesses that it brings, and, most of all, let that child know you love him just the way God created him.

Teach Your Child That He Is Valuable

Many loving parents make the mistake of giving their children the impression they don't measure up. Condemnation, recrimination, and faultfinding tell your child that you wish he were

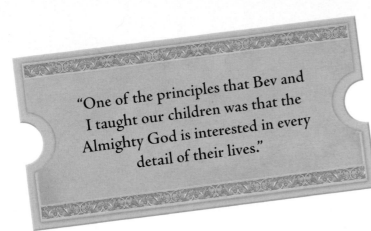

"One of the principles that Bev and I taught our children was that the Almighty God is interested in every detail of their lives."

different. Some parents even verbalize their disapproval. You can imagine what that does to a child's self-esteem.

Imagine little eight-year-old Johnny looking up at Mom and Dad with big, liquid eyes, pleading, "Please love me, as I am."

"Shouldn't you be doing your homework?" you ask impatiently.

All you can think about is, *How will he ever get accepted into college if his grades don't improve? Only God could make anything good out of him.*

He turns away slowly, thinking, *If my parents don't think I'll ever amount to anything I guess I never will.*

That's why it is so important to give our approval and love unconditionally — with no strings attached. Sure, correct their mistakes and the things they do wrong, but always tell them, "I believe God is in the manufacturing business, and He can take your unique gifts and talents and use them for His glory."

Always remember, God has a wonderful plan for your child's life.

TEACH YOUR CHILDREN THAT GOD ANSWERS PRAYER

One of the principles that Bev and I taught our children was that Almighty God is interested in every detail of their lives. We did this not only by studying God's Word together but also by living it.

One Christmas Bev and I were visiting with my married daughter and her family. While walking through the kitchen, I noticed a bulletin board, where they had posted prayer requests. Down in the right hand corner was a picture of a blue Jeep Cherokee.

I knew they'd been having trouble with one of their cars, and that it was time for a new one. When I saw that picture, I couldn't help but laugh. My mind raced back 20 years when our daughter was young.

On our prayer board, we had posted a picture of a red Plymouth station wagon. With four kids, two parents, and neighbor kids going to Sunday school, our family needed the biggest car we could find. At that time, it was the nine-passenger station wagon. I found one in a magazine, and we began praying.

I had been teaching my kids, "In all your ways acknowledge Him, And He shall direct your paths" (Prov. 3:6). In other words, God will supply all your needs. "Knock, and seek, and ask," I told them. After praying for two months, the kids began to think God wasn't listening.

Then one Thursday night — I'll never forget it — the phone rang. It was a deacon from a Baptist church 35 miles across town. I'd never met him, but he worked with a man from our church who knew about our transportation problem. The deacon said, "I understand you're looking for a new car."

"How did you know we were looking for a car?"

When I said "car," the whole house shut down. Every ear tuned in to that conversation.

"I'm in the Navy," he told me, "and I'm being shipped back to Virginia Beach. I have a car I want to sell."

"Well," I began, "I must tell you right up front, I don't have any money for a down payment."

He said, "That's okay, I just need somebody to take over the payments."

"Well, I'm limited on how much I can spend," I replied "We could only afford $100 a month."

"My payments are $105."

Now, I was interested! "What kind of a car is it?"

"It's a Plymouth station wagon."

My throat went dry, and it was so quiet in the house that I found myself holding my breath.

"How many seats does it have?"

I knew Plymouth also made a two-seat station wagon.

"It's a nine passenger, three-seat station wagon."

Then I really got nervous and asked, "What color is it?"

Long pause. Then he said, "Pastor LaHaye, I almost didn't call you because knowing that you're a minister, I didn't think you'd want a red one."

"A red one!" I shouted, and the whole house went wild.

We rushed over there, did all the paperwork, brought the car home, and all six of us sat in the driveway as we dedicated that car to the Lord.

We enjoyed that station wagon for seven years. In fact, when our kids think back on their childhood, they think of that family car.

Twenty years go by, and my daughter and her family need a car, and so what do they do? Put a picture on the prayer board, believing that God watches and He hears.

Not long after that visit I called my daughter and said, "I'm coming in to San Diego. Would you come by and pick me up at the airport?"

"Sure, Dad, what time are you coming?"

I said, "4:30."

"Oh, good, the kids want to see you when you see it."

I said, "Oh, what is it?"

"I can't tell you. I'm sworn to secrecy."

Guess what "it" was? A blue, four-wheel drive Jeep Cherokee.

Let me ask you a question. Do you think my grandkids think God answers prayers? We've taught them to pray for cars, motorcycles, college, jobs, houses — everything. Why? So their joy can be full, just as God promised (John 15:11).

Teach Your Kids the Secret of Happiness

Parade magazine polled thousands of teenagers and asked them what they most wanted in life. The largest number — 28 percent — said their first desire was happiness; second was a long and enjoyable life. Those two together come to almost 50 percent. The teens' third desire was for marriage and family.

What about a great career? You know, what are you going to do with your life? Surprisingly, that goal ranked only sixth.

Everyone wants happiness.

Happiness is the result of obeying God's principles. How do I know? Because the Bible tells me so.

The psalmist David said, "Happy" or "blessed are the undefiled in the way, Who walk in the law of the Lord!" (Ps. 119:1). Jesus said, "Blessed are those who hear the word of God and keep it!" (Luke 11:28). "If you know these things," — His principles — Jesus said, "blessed are you if you do them" (John 13:17).

Who are the happiest people in the world? The rich and famous? I think not. The self-seekers live in abject misery. God created man morally conscious and responsible to be a servant. It is not the masters but the servants who enjoy happiness. If you serve God, He will bless your life.

The humanist's world view offers no hope: "When you're dead, you're dead. That's it." The Christian, however, sees this world as a temporary residence, a field that is white unto harvest.

We want to serve Christ by reaching people with the message of salvation as Jesus commanded us: "Go into all the world and preach the gospel" (Mark 16:15). That goal gives us a lifetime motivation and a purpose for living.

The biblical world view is one of hope that offers life after death. Jesus said, "I go to prepare a place for you. . . . I will come again and receive you to Myself; that where I am, there you may be also" (John 14:2-3). What a wonderful hope!

When we die, we live! We go to a much better place. Best of all, Jesus will be there. Who could ask for anything more? That's the most important principle your children will ever learn.

Your Best Gift to Your Children

During the 25 years I pastored in San Diego we had a tremendous youth program, an outgrowth of the ministry of Jerry Riffe, who served with me for 23 years, and other youth pastors. We estimate that about 300 young people answered the call of God to go into some kind of Christian work during those years.

After I resigned and before I left, I asked Jerry what kind of homes the Christian workers came out of. He replied, "We have three kinds of homes in our church." Then he listed the following:

1. *Spirit-filled families most of the time, and the majority come from these homes.*
2. *Carnal Christian homes — they almost never come out of those families.*
3. *Unsaved or mixed, where only one parent was a Christian — they sometimes come out of these families.*

I challenged him on that, thinking as pastors do that regular church families, yes, even Christian leader's families, would produce better fruit than mixed or unsaved families.

"No," he said, "if Dad is unsaved and acts like a pagan at home, the kids can understand. But if he is a leader in the church and acts like a pagan at home, that is hypocrisy. Young people can't handle that! Which is why they rarely if ever come from such families and go into Christian work."

The best thing you can give your mate and your family is a Spirit-filled mother and father — it will affect their entire life!

Some have said that our culture today is depraved. We acknowledge that, while keeping in mind that there are still good, faithful people in our land.

Amazingly, Paul had the spiritual discernment to "see" into the future and understand that as the world increased its rejection of God, the young people would be among the most vulnerable. We can see this in his letters to Timothy.

Are you aware of what your child sees on television? The airwaves are full of "reality" shows (that, ironically, have no basis in reality!) in which teens and 20-somethings degrade themselves in the hopes they will be discovered by directors, music producers, etc. None of it is edifying. Consider how these shows contrast with God's teaching for families and relationships.

On an given program today, you will see a self-absorbed young man given the task of choosing a wife from among a dozen or more young women. The goal of this type of show is to win at all costs. Those trying to win will go to any lengths, including lying, cheating, and stealing.

You might notice, too, if you care to look, that Saturday morning cartoons are no longer dominated by clever rabbits with Brooklyn accents, moral super heroes, and harmless characters children can relate to. No, almost all programming today, magazines, internet sites, and video games are the domain of immoral characters who are influencing families.

Purpose in your hearts and in your homes to follow the only true guide for life. God's word is as relevant as ever, no matter what its critics say. Determine to stand against the soul-killing pursuits of entertainment industries and give your family spiritual health.

That's the only reality that will bring you peace and joy!

Photo Credits